# Priority Number One in Prayer

## The Key to Revival

Fred Lambert

ISBN-13: 978-1-7326263-0-0

# DEDICATION

This book is dedicated to Jesus Christ and His beautiful Bride!

# CONTENTS

# ACKNOWLEDGMENTS

Thanks to Jesus for saving me, loving me and never giving up on me. Thanks to my beautiful wife Judy who inspires me to be a better man. Thanks to my children and grandchildren who are running faster, building bigger and accomplishing more than me. Thanks to Brother Kenneth E. Hagin, Pastor Gerritt Kenyon and Pastor David Ingles who taught me so much about prayer and walking in love.

# INTRODUCTION

What you are about to read came as a revelation.

Let me explain.

A number of years ago we started an early morning prayer meeting in our church. When I first announced it to our congregation, among other things I said,

"… and I will be there every morning."

After the church service that morning I *realized* what I had said. I had just committed myself to being there every time!

My first thought was, "Why did I say I'd be there every time? Why didn't I just say that someone from our pastoral team would be there every time?"

I'm really not that much of a morning person! But now the whole congregation would hold me accountable! There was no getting around it and no getting out of it.

I had to be there.

Every time.

Guess what my first thought was the next morning when the alarm went off?

That's right – you guessed it!

"Why did I say I'd be there every time? Why didn't I just say that someone from our pastoral team would be there every time?"

I didn't have goose bumps and I wasn't feeling extra spiritual when the alarm rang. Actually, I just wanted to shut the alarm off and go back to sleep! But I had to get up. I had committed myself! So, not feeling overly spiritual, I got up, got ready and went to the church.

When I got there,
    I greeted the people
        opened my Bible
            read a scripture about prayer
                said a few words about it
                    and then we prayed for an hour.

Nothing exceptional happened. Don't get me wrong. It was a good time of prayer and God blessed us with His presence but it was nothing unusual. Prayer should always be a good time and we should always experience His presence in prayer.

That's the norm!

During our prayer time – along with other things – we prayed the prayers of Paul found in his letters to the Ephesians and the Colossians. We prayed them for ourselves, for our church and for the body of Christ.

Paul prayed that God would give them the spirit of wisdom and revelation in the KNOWLEDGE of God. He prayed that the eyes of their hearts would be ENLIGHTENED. He prayed that they would KNOW the love of Christ, which passes knowledge. He prayed that they would be filled with all spiritual WISDOM and UNDERSTANDING!

These are prayers for revelation knowledge.

Like I said, it was a good prayer time but nothing exceptional happened. Nothing unusual. Nothing sensational. Just a good, normal time of prayer.

When the alarm went off the next morning guess what my first thought was – again!

Yep! You got it!

2

"Why did I say I'd be there every time?" Argh!

But I got up,
    got ready,
        drove to church,
            greeted the people,
                read a prayer scripture,
                    said a few words about it
                        and then we prayed for an hour.

And again, it was a good time, God's presence was there but nothing spectacular or unusual happened. Do you know what I mean by that?

Sometimes there are things we experience in prayer that are MEGA-life-changing and unique. Sometimes we hear things from God or He helps us in a certain way that is extra *special*. Something happens that brings us up to the next level of spiritual development!

And then there are other times – most of the times – where it's good and wonderful but it's just the normal kind of good and wonderful. We talk to Him. He talks to us. Prayers are answered. We're blessed. That's how it was that day.

Guess what my first thought was on the third day?

    "Why did I say I'd be there every time?"
        On the fourth day?
            Right. Again. Yep.
            Etc.

But I got up, got ready and went to early morning prayer.

Day after day, we had good times of prayer and enjoyed God's wonderful presence. We also received answers to our prayers. It was good every time.

Normal good.

Oh, and by the way– and we prayed the Ephesians and Colossians prayers for ourselves, for our church and for the body of Christ every time.

After a while I got used to getting up early and going to the church for prayer. I stopped asking, "Why did I say that" and was actually glad that I had said it.

Sometimes we need to commit ourselves and make ourselves accountable to others! It's good and healthy as well as being totally biblical. Don't believe the people who say that accountability is bondage or legalism.

### It's not.

Anyhow, about two months after we started, something unusual happened. Something exceptional, unique and life changing happened!

I experienced what I can only describe as a breakthrough into revelation knowledge.

The alarm went off,
   I got up,
      got ready,
         went to church,
            opened my Bible,
               read a scripture
               and

BOOM!

This time it was different. This time it was exceptional. This time it was spectacular.

I began to see things that I had never seen before. Scripture opened up to me in a new way. Truths that had always been there – written on those precious pages – began to illuminate my spirit and my mind. The eyes of my heart were being enlightened. God was showing me things.

This book is the product of one of those revelations.

Don't misunderstand me. I am not speaking of an "extra-biblical" revelation. I believe, just as much as you, that the Bible is a closed Canon – we shouldn't add to or take away from it.

But the Bible is a supernatural book. It's inexhaustible in depth.

There are so many things that we have yet to see, so many truths we have yet to fathom. No one has plumbed the deepest depths of God's word except God Himself!

And there are special times when He shares with us one of those hidden treasures in His word. He opens our spiritual eyes. He pulls back the curtain and shows us "great and mighty things" which we didn't know!

***Jeremiah 33:3*** *Call to Me, and I will answer you, and show you great and mighty things, which you do not know.*

The prayers in Paul's letter to the Ephesians point to this.

He writes by inspiration of the Holy Spirit.
　　He trusts that his letter will be delivered to the church.
　　　　He knows they will read these Holy Spirit inspired words.

And yet he prays that God would give them the Spirit of wisdom and revelation. In other words, the letter alone is not enough.

It's as if Paul said, "I am sending you words that I received from the Holy Spirit. I know that you can read what I have written with pen, ink and paper. But friends, you're going to need God's help to really understand the message. You'll have to have the Spirit of wisdom and revelation to really get it."

There are some truths that are just too big for our mental capacities to comprehend.

There is a **LOVE** so big that it surpasses knowledge.
　　There is a **JOY** that's unspeakable and full of glory.
　　　　There is a perfect **PEACE** that passes understanding.

Words simply don't exist in human language that can convey the depths of these things. We can't completely fathom them with our limited mental faculties!

We need revelation. We need the Holy Spirit to help us understand the word of God. Thank God that He lives in every believer. The Author of the Bible Himself, lives in us and will teach us all things.

I believe that the truth I'm sharing in this book is so powerful that it could genuinely transform your life, your church, the body of Christ and even the world. I really believe that! But you will need the help of the Holy Spirit to truly get it.

The amazing thing about this truth is that it is so simple. It is so simple in fact, that it is often overlooked. Even with all the great teaching that we have today, this truth is rarely mentioned and has never received the attention that it deserves!

I began to see that God's Word emphasizes a specific *priority* in prayer. It is found all throughout the New Testament but it is seldom – if ever – mentioned in the great conferences, teaching seminars, books or published materials that we have on the subject of prayer.

I call this revelation, "Priority Number One in Prayer".

You'll probably be surprised when you see how much the Bible actually says about this simple truth. I know I was.

I am persuaded that if the church grasps this truth and acts upon it, things will change for the better – for all of us – and for the world.

Sounds big, doesn't it?

It is.

It is priority number one in prayer!

# Priority Number One in Prayer

# 1. PRIORITY NUMBER ONE IN PRAYER

*Ephesians 6:18 praying always with all prayer and supplication in the Spirit, being watchful to this end with all perseverance and supplication for all the saints.*

This is one of my favorite prayer scriptures. I had probably read it or heard it more than a hundred times before I finally saw what I'm now sharing with you.

I heard sermons about it and even preached about it myself.

In **Ephesians 6:18** we are called to:

> Pray all kinds of prayer
> > in the Spirit,
> > > be watchful
> > > > and persevere.

It's a good outline! That'll preach!

But on that morning, it was like the last four words of this verse jumped off the page and came alive to me. Those four words are:

## "for all the saints"

We are told to pray all kinds of prayer, all the time, in the spirit and to persevere in supplication *"for all the saints."*

Get it? Paul tells us to pray for the saints, aka (also known as) believers. Perhaps no one has ever accused you of being a saint but if you're in Christ you are one! Some churches have patron saints and canonize certain people that they consider worthy of sainthood. But if you're born again, Jesus has already canonized you! You are a saint. God has made you righteous by the blood of Jesus.

**2 Corinthians 5:21** For He made Him who knew no sin to be sin for us, that we might become the righteousness of God in Him.

Praying "for all the saints" means praying for Christians.

Much has been said about
    praying for the lost,
        praying for the government,
           praying for the nations,
           praying for Israel,
               praying for our own needs,
                  praying in other tongues
                and so on.

All of these things are good and important but the New Testament has a lot more to say about praying for the body of Christ than it does about praying for anything else.

Yes, we should pray for the lost, for the government, for the nations, for Israel, for our needs and so on. But praying for our brothers and sisters in Christ is far more important than ALL of that! Praying for the body of Christ is priority number one in prayer".

At least according to the New Testament it is!

**Romans 8:26-27** *Likewise the Spirit also helps in our weaknesses. For we do not know what we should pray for as we ought, but the Spirit Himself makes intercession for us with groanings which cannot be uttered. 27 Now He who searches the hearts knows what the mind of the Spirit is, because He makes intercession for the saints according to the will of God.*

This scripture has been used to teach entire seminars on the "spirit of prayer" and how to effectively intercede for the lost.

People like
    Charles Finney,
        Father Daniel Nash,
            David Brainerd,
                Maria Woodsworth-Etter,
                    John Hyde
                        Evan Roberts,
                            Reese Howells,
                                William Seymour
                                    and a host of others

are often mentioned as examples of those who had the true spirit of prayer.

We're told of how they made intercession for the lost with groans and deep sighs. They "wrestled" with God. They cried out, "Give me souls or I'll die." I love those stories. These men and women of God had tremendous experiences with God. They won multitudes for the Lord! They are faith heroes! I am not worthy to tie their shoes!

And don't get me wrong. Interceding in prayer for the lost is very important! But that's not what this scripture is talking about. Look at those three important words in verse 27:

### "for the saints"

In **Romans 8:26-27**, Paul is not talking about interceding for the lost but rather for believers! Rarely is this scripture used to teach about praying for the saints but that's exactly what Paul is talking about. Praying for the body of Christ is granted a priority in the New Testament that overshadows praying for anything else!

I know that this may sound new to you. It was for me.

Perhaps you're thinking, "What can be more important than praying for the lost? Without Jesus they will spend eternity separated from God!"

That's true! But prayers do not save the lost!

The lost will not be saved until they hear the gospel, believe it and receive Jesus as their Lord. And the job of preaching the Gospel has been entrusted to the saints – to believers – to Christians – to the body of Christ.

If we don't do our job, then many will not hear and many will not be saved. This is why prayer for the body of Christ is so important! We have a job to do and we need God's help – and each other's help to do it!

When we read the New Testament we are continually told to pray for one another. But nowhere are we specifically told to pray for the lost. In fact, there is only one scripture that says anything about praying that the lost would be saved.

**Romans 10:1** Brethren, my heart's desire and prayer to God for Israel is, that they might be saved.

Paul prayed that the unbelieving Jews would be saved. He doesn't give us any instructions at all about how he did this. He doesn't even tell us that *we* should do this. The only thing that he tells us is that he prayed for Israel "that they might be saved."

And yet there are intercession groups, books and prayer manuals about how to pray for Israel. Sadly, some of these groups and materials have very little to say about praying for the saints or praying for believers.

The Apostle Paul however – the  guy who wrote Romans 10:1 – a Hebrew of the Hebrews – said MUCH more about praying for the church than he did about praying for Israel.

And again, he really didn't even tell us that *WE* should pray for Israel!

Selah! (Pause and think about that.)

… still pausing …

Ok, good! Should we pray for Israel?

Emphatically YES! Praying for Israel is good and right.

If Israel had only one friend in the whole wide world it should be us – the body of Christ. We have a shared history and inheritance. We worship the God of Abraham, Isaac and Jacob. We received the Bible through the Jews. Jesus is the Lion of the Tribe of Judah, the Messiah, the King of the Jews!

Yes, we should pray for Israel!
Yes, we should love Israel!
Yes, we should support Israel!

But praying for the body of Christ is far more important. If the body of Christ is not strong and fulfilling the commission that Jesus committed to us, then our prayers for Israel will have little effect.

We could pray for the peace of Jerusalem until we're blue in the face and get no results! The Bible tells us that there will be no real peace in Jerusalem until Jesus, the Prince of Peace returns! And that will not happen until we get our job done! Yes, we should pray for Israel but we should pray like Paul did – "that they might be saved!"

Some Christians have become so blinded by inter-religious correctness that they're not even preaching the Gospel to the Jews anymore. But friend, you can be sure of this, without faith in Jesus Christ, no one will be saved. Neither Jew nor Gentile stands a chance without Him. All are lost. All have sinned. He alone can wash away the sin and guilt that condemns lost sinners. Jesus Himself said, *"I am the way, the truth and the life. No one comes to the Father except through Me."* (**John 14:6**)

Paul did indeed pray for the unbelieving Jews but he also preached the Gospel to them. And when it came to prayer, praying for believers was priority number one in Paul's prayer life. (We'll take a closer look at that in the next pages.)

There are way too many Christians who are sick, suffering, weak, poor, depressed, beaten down and living defeated lives.

Marriages are falling apart under the attack of the enemy. Financial ruin is threatening many. Multitudes of believers are ineffective in their witness for Christ. God's people are being destroyed because of a lack of revelation knowledge. This is not the will of God for His children!

We are called to be light to the world and salt to the earth. (**Matthew 5:13-16**) We are called to be witnesses; testifying that Jesus is alive. (**Acts 1:8**) We are called to show forth the praises of Him who has called us out of darkness into His marvelous light. (**2 Peter 2:9**)

But many of us are distracted and paralyzed by our own problems and issues. Many of us are living lives that are no different than unbelievers. Many of us are too weak spiritually and afraid to speak up for Jesus. And it breaks my heart to say it but others are so confused that they can't testify with conviction about anything!

We need prayer.
We need one another.
We need to pray for one another.
This must become the priority it's meant to be!

There are brothers and sisters in our churches right now who are in desperate need of the help that we can give them through our prayers.

Prayer is powerful!
Prayer helps!
Prayer changes things.

Paul realized how powerful and helpful the prayers of the church were for his ministry. In writing to the church at Corinth he said, *"God has delivered us from such a deadly peril, and he will deliver us. On him we have set our hope that he will continue to deliver us, as you help us by your prayers. (**2 Corinthians 1:10-11a NIV**)*

He knew that their prayers were helping him fulfill God's plan for His life and ministry!

James wrote, *"The effectual fervent prayer of a righteous person avails much!"* (**James 5:16**)

Prayer releases God's power into the lives of those for whom we pray.

Through prayer we can:
> strengthen those who are weak,
>> restore health to those who are sick,
>>> obtain blessing for those who suffer lack,
>>>> help one another as we witness for Jesus and
>>>>> release the wisdom and revelation needed
>>>>>> to live victoriously in Christ.
>>>>>> .

Let's begin to help one another in prayer.

Some intercession groups emphasize things like spiritual warfare, changing the destiny of nations through intercession or praying out the deep mysteries of God's plan. All of that may be fine and good but these things will do little or no good if the body of Christ is weak, beaten down and defeated.

True *spiritual warfare* requires a strong army of believers to go out and set the captives free by preaching, teaching, casting out demons and healing the sick!

The *destiny of nations* will never be changed until the body of Christ is operating according to revelation knowledge and strengthened with might by His Spirit!

Discovering and fulfilling *God's plan* for OUR lives is greatly dependent upon other believers discovering and fulfilling God's plan for THEIR lives.

**1 Corinthians 12:26** *And if one member suffers, all the members suffer with it; or if one member is honored, all the members rejoice with it.*

We are one body. We need each other.
> My success, is in part, dependent on your success.
>> Your success, is in part, dependent on my success.
>> If you are suffering, I am suffering.

The problem is that we often don't see how much we ALL are suffering. We are so consumed with our own lives, problems and challenges that we just don't recognize the suffering of our brothers and sisters. Much of this suffering has nothing to do with the will of God and could be averted by prayer! Whether we realize it or not, this is having an exponentially negative impact on the whole body of Christ.

If one suffers, we all suffer.
If millions suffer, we all suffer much!

We need our brothers and sisters to be strong, Spirit-filled and operating in the grace that God has granted them. The great work to which He has called us REQUIRES it!

*John 14:20 At that day you will know that I am in My Father, and you in Me, and I in you.*

I am in Christ. He is in me.
    You are in Christ. He is in you.
        I am in Him. He is in you.
            You are in Him. He is in me.
                **I am in Him – in you!**
                **You are in Him – in me!**
                **We are in each other!**

We need each other's prayer support just as much as our body needs the next beat of our heart! Praying for the body of Christ is "priority number one" in New Testament prayer.

Not convinced? Read on

# 2. PRAYING FOR ALL MEN

*1 Timothy 2:1-4 Therefore I exhort first of all that supplications, prayers, intercessions, and giving of thanks be made for all men, 2 for kings and all who are in authority, that we may lead a quiet and peaceable life in all godliness and reverence. 3 For this is good and acceptable in the sight of God our Savior, 4 who desires all men to be saved and to come to the knowledge of the truth.*

Earlier I said that there are very few scriptures in the New Testament that mention anything at all about praying for the lost.

That's true.
There are only three.

The scripture above is one of those passages. But even here, it doesn't specifically say we should pray for the lost. The lost would be included here because the term "all men" refers to all people including those who do not yet believe in Jesus. A solid hermeneutical, exegetical inspection of this passage combined with a merely nominal understanding of Judeo-Christian, theological anthropology reveals that this also is a prayer for believers! ☺ In other words, "all men" includes believers or Christians as well as unbelievers.

The "first of all" in this verse has led some to believe that we should pray first and foremost for kings or for the government.

**Not so.**

Although praying for international, national and local leaders of government is important, Paul is not saying that we should pray first of all for them.

Here's why:

First of all, the *"first of all"* in this scripture is not a call to pray "first of all" for the government. In this case, "first of all" does not denote a priority in prayer.

The first thing that he "first of all" mentions is praying "for all men" or "all people." He includes kings *after* "all people" *not before*. If we are to understand any kind of priority here, it is that before serving, doing, working, preaching, teaching and so on, we should pray for the people we are to serve.

Everything should begin with prayer. Prayer paves the way for miracles! In the book of Acts, every great harvest of souls, every miracle, every healing and every deliverance was prefaced with prayer! Never forget it, to minister effectively everything begins with prayer.

Actually, the "first of all" in this scripture is simply the opening of Paul's practical instructions to Timothy. This would be the equivalent of saying, "To begin with, let me say…"

Secondly, check out the reason he says that we should pray for kings and all who are in authority:

*"That **we** might lead a quiet and peaceable life in all godliness and honesty."*

> **We pray for them – for us.**
> **Let me say that again.**
> **We pray for them – for us.**

We pray for the leaders of governments because what they do can impact the lives of believers. Indirectly, praying for those in civil authority should result in blessing for the body of Christ.

And it will - *if* we pray in faith.

Years ago I attended a prayer meeting with other pastors. It was at a time when most Christians in the country where I live thought that the wrong people had been elected. The brother who led the prayer meeting told us of the dangers of the new coalition and of how our country would suffer. He was worried and afraid that bad things would happen and he called on us to pray.

So we prayed
    for the government
        for about 15 – 20 minutes
            and then we all said,
                "Amen."

After we finished praying, the brother who called on us to pray started complaining and criticizing the new government all over again. I sighed inwardly and thought to myself, "We just wasted our time." Anything we had accomplished in prayer was torn to smithereens by his unbelief.

Jesus said, "All things you ask in prayer, believing, you will receive".

After we pray, we should give thanks – not complain and criticize. If we believe that God has heard and answered our prayer we should be grateful – not worried and afraid! Faith gives thanks because it knows that God has heard and answered our prayer!

And just a side thought, the next time someone starts criticizing and complaining about the government – ask them how much they've prayed for them. Ask them if they've thanked God for hearing and answering their prayers.

If they have any sense, they'll stop complaining.

Someone once said, "Complainers are not pray-ers and pray-ers are not complainers." I believe that. Paul told us to pray and give thanks, not pray and complain. Just sayin'.

Anyway – we pray for kings and all who are in authority so that the body of Christ will be blessed. Paul lists two main reasons why this is important.

First of all... ☺

"For this is good and acceptable in the sight of God our Savior."

We should pray for the government so that the body of Christ will be blessed because it pleases God when His people are blessed!

Did you know that?
Some Christians don't.

One man said to me sarcastically, "Apparently Paul didn't know that because he had hard times wherever he went!"

Nice.

Thanks a lot buddy!
You're a great help!

What he said sounds good and religious but it's also misleading. It'd be a great help if people like that would just read the Bible – the whole thing – in context – without their religious bifocals.

Did Paul have hard times? Yes. But why did he have hard times? There are several reasons – reasons found right in the Bible. But they are not the reasons implied by my dear brother's comment.

In his thinking, it couldn't be God's will to bless His children because Paul experienced hard times. The problem with this "logic" is that we can't build our faith on anyone else's experiences – not even Paul's!

We build our faith on God's instructions and promises.

The whole Bible is inspired by the Holy Spirit but that doesn't mean that every story and experience we read in the Bible reveals God's perfect will for our lives. We have to interpret these stories and experiences in the light of the clear teaching passages in the Bible. If not, we may wind up with false conclusions.

For example, if we based our faith entirely on Paul's life and experiences then none of us should be married. He wasn't. And all men should be circumcised. He was.

But in the teaching passages of his own letters we see that neither of these personal life experiences are God's will for all people.

*1 Corinthians 7:7 For I wish that all men were even as I myself. But each one has his own gift from God, one in this manner and another in that.*

*Galatians 6:15 For in Christ Jesus neither circumcision nor uncircumcision avails anything, but a new creation.*

So getting back to the point, the statement "it can't please God to bless His children because Paul experienced hard times" just doesn't fly! We don't base our faith on Paul's experiences but rather on the clear teaching passages of the Bible.

It'd actually be hypocritical for anyone to claim Paul's hardships as the basis for their own unless they have left everything behind for the sake of the Gospel. That's what he did and that's one of the reasons that he experienced so many hard times.

He said that he denied himself of rights and privileges that he was entitled to. (**1 Corinthians 9:1-18**) He also said that it seemed to him as if God put the apostles on display as the least of all and as those condemned to death. (**1 Corinthians 4:9-13**)

Those who claim Paul's sufferings as the basis for their hard times must think that they are apostles in the league of Paul.

And they're not.

Every one of us will experience suffering at times but not all suffering is according to the will of God.

Two kinds of suffering can be categorized as "suffering according to the will of God". (**1 Peter 4:19**) One of them is persecution as we boldly witness for Christ and the other is self-denial as we pursue holiness. All other forms of suffering are not in accordance with the will of God. Suffering because of our own mistakes or rebellion is not the will of God nor is suffering sickness, poverty, loneliness, depression or a host of other things we could list.

And none of that changes the fact that Paul said we should "pray for kings and all in authority that we might live a quiet and peaceful life in all godliness and reverence". Why are we to pray this? Because it pleases God when His children are blessed!

The Christian life is a blessed life, not a cursed life.

*Galatians 3:13-14 Christ has redeemed us from the curse of the law, having become a curse for us (for it is written, "Cursed is everyone who hangs on a tree"), 14 that the blessing of Abraham might come upon the Gentiles in Christ Jesus, that we might receive the promise of the Spirit through faith.*

Jesus took the curse that we deserved and gave us the blessing we didn't deserve! The blessing of Abraham now belongs to all who are in Christ! What is the blessing of Abraham?

*Genesis 12:2-3 I will make you a great nation; I will bless you And make your name great; And you shall be a blessing. 3 I will bless those who bless you, And I will curse him who curses you; And in you all the families of the earth shall be blessed."*

The blessing that God promised Abraham was a blessing for every area of his life – spirit, soul and body! It was for him, his wife and his whole family! He was going to be so blessed that he could be a blessing to all the families of the earth! You've got to be pretty blessed to do that! And this blessing is now ours in Christ.

What did this blessing do for Abraham? A lot! Among other things, the blessing made him rich.

**Genesis 13:2** Abram was very rich in livestock, in silver, and in gold.

If all the families of the earth are going to be blessed through Abraham and now through us as his offspring and heirs, then Abraham and all of us are going to have to be pretty blessed!

Sure, people have perverted and abused the biblical teaching about financial blessing and prosperity but that doesn't mean we should ignore everything that God said about it in the Bible.

You will always find extremes when it comes to theological views.

One man of God said, "It seems to be the hardest thing in the world for Christians to stay in the middle of the road".

Yep.

You'll find people off balance or in the ditch on one side of the road or the other when it comes to finances – and other subjects too.

Some people say that God doesn't care at all about how we're doing financially. They claim that in the New Testament, God is only interested in our spiritual well-being. (Apparently they can't read very well.)

There are more scriptures in the Bible about finances than there are about faith. God apparently cares more about our financial well-being and our attitude concerning finances than some people think.

You'll even hear some folks praise poverty as if it were a noble, spiritual virtue. Perhaps they should ask the parents of children who are starving to death if they think poverty is a noble, spiritual virtue. Then they should ask Jesus why He told us to feed and clothe the poor, hungry and naked!

The people in this ditch make it sound like poverty is a prerequisite to walking in holiness and humility! But God is very rich, very holy and very humble! He humbled Himself and took on the form of a slave!

Such notions are foolish and found nowhere in scripture. How is the body of Christ going to feed the poor, clothe the naked, send out missionaries and build churches if we can't even feed ourselves?

Neither poverty nor prosperity are foolproof evidences of spirituality, humility or a lack thereof.

Two things are clear, however. Prosperity is often referred to as a blessing of God in the Bible, but poverty *never* is. Poverty is *always* referred to as a curse!

It's sad and true that some preachers have abused and misused God's promises of financial blessing for their own personal gain. Some have manipulated and hoodwinked God's gullible children to give into their "ministry" by misrepresenting Scripture and using pressure tactics. People have been taken advantage of, deceived, duped and hurt by such "preachers".

Yes, that's wrong.
Yes, that's a problem.

But don't worry about them – no one ever gets away with anything. Pray for them because if they don't repent they're going to get into big trouble – either now or later.

And let's not throw the baby out with the bathwater because of the extremes or because of the people in the ditches on either side of the road!

God wants to bless us and make us a blessing to all the families on the earth! If we want to feed the poor, clothe the naked, support missionaries and build churches we are going to have to have some money to do it.

What does that have to do with our subject? Glad you asked! Let's get back to it.

Paul said that we should pray for the government so that we can live a "quiet and peaceable life". That's what God wants for His people and our prayers can make it happen! A quiet and peaceable life is not a life of struggle, worry and lack!

The words for "quiet" and "peaceable" in the Greek New Testament have a very similar meaning. The word "quiet" is "eremos" and the word "peaceable" is "hesuchios". (Don't you feel like you're a better person now just by knowing that? ☺) "Vine's Expository Dictionary of Biblical Words" explains the subtle difference in meaning of the two words. "Eremos" indicates a tranquility arising from without and "hesuchios" indicates a tranquility arising from within.

The quiet and peaceable life is one where we are blessed inwardly and outwardly.

Pray for the government, that the political, social and economic conditions will be optimal for the church and her mission. Pray that believers will have favor and prosper inwardly and outwardly. Pray that they will have everything they need – spiritually and materially – to fulfill the call of God on their lives!

And maybe pray that they won't be selfish and greedy after God blesses them! ☺

If Paul's hardships are meant to be our example in all things, then we should immediately leave our possessions, homes and families and go preach the Gospel where Christ has not yet been named.

That's what he did.

I'm sure that if you do that, you will experience some of the hardships that he did. Try going to Afghanistan and preaching there, for example. I have heroic friends that are doing just that and believe me, it's not easy.

But again, we're not supposed to build our faith upon anyone else's experiences! You aren't called to be Paul. You have your gift and he had his gift. If you try to walk in his gift you'll most likely just stay dead after they stone you! ☺

The hardships Paul experienced weren't just material they were spiritual. Much of his suffering was brought about by persecution and persecution is promised to all who will live godly lives in Christ. (If you're not experiencing persecution, now you know why.)

If we're truly serving God we will experience some persecution. But that doesn't mean that we will be sick, broke and homeless!

Jesus told His disciples, "*Assuredly, I say to you, there is no one who has left house or brothers or sisters or father or mother or wife or children or lands, for My sake and the gospel's, who shall not receive a hundredfold now in this time — houses and brothers* *and sisters and mothers and children and lands, with persecutions — and in the age to come, eternal life." **Mark 10:29-30***

It almost seems like a contradiction in terms.

Those who follow Jesus wholly will be both blessed and persecuted. At times we may be called upon to deny ourselves of our rights and privileges. That was Paul's life. But he wasn't always broke. He wasn't a pauper. He experienced times of abundance and times of lack. The seasons of lack were often the result of his unique call and his extreme dedication and zeal to that call.

He forfeited his rights for the sake of others! He obeyed the call to go where Christ was unnamed. He chose to leave his career, his family, his friends and his home church and go for God!

He was blessed but persecuted.
He was rich and yet at times poor.
He sacrificed and gave his all for the gospel.

But that was his call.
That was his gifting.
That was his course.

The vast majority of believers are not called to leave their careers, families, friends and home churches. And that's not just my opinion, that's what Paul said by inspiration of the Holy Spirit.

***1 Corinthians 7:17** Nevertheless, each one should retain the place in life that the Lord assigned to him and to which God has called him. This is the rule I lay down in all the churches.*

***1 Corinthians 7:20** Each one should remain in the situation which he was in when God called him.*

The majority of us are called to be witnesses right where we are and support our churches in taking the Gospel to our communities and to the ends of the earth. We are not called to take a vow of poverty. We are called to live in the blessings that Jesus purchased for us and to bless as many people as we possibly can!

And at times we will be persecuted.

Being blessed doesn't necessarily mean that you will always be rich and financially comfortable. There are a number of factors mentioned in the Bible that influence our financial condition. We cannot ignore these principles and expect to walk in God's blessing in this area.

Financial prosperity is a blessing and can be used to further the gospel but God may call us, as He did Paul, to deny ourselves of our rights and privileges and go to work among the unreached people groups of the world. If so, we will never experience greater blessing than in obeying God's call!

But if that isn't your call – and again, for the majority of people it isn't – then I want to encourage you to walk in all the blessings that God purchased for you in Christ. I want to encourage you to use those blessings for reaching the lost and building the kingdom of God.

Sure – eat good, stay healthy, have a happy family life, enjoy your job, live in a nice house, drive a nice car but ABOVE ALL ELSE, give and do as much as you can for the work of the gospel.

That's what the blessing is for.

Don't let the hyper-prosperity or anti-prosperity preachers confuse you! Get into the word for yourself and stay balanced!

Some of them are nothing more than propagandists for their denominations and theological viewpoints. Several famous anti-prosperity preachers are very rich. They have made millions from their books, TV shows and "ministries". One of them (who I won't name) has a base salary of more than $500,000.00 per year! The anti-prosperity market is pretty big and can be a very profitable business.

On the other hand there are hyper-prosperity preachers who look rich on the outside but are broke and in debt. They keep preaching their unbalanced message to finance their big houses, cars and TV time.

Let's pray for all of them to come to their senses. Or better yet, pray that they repent of their foolishness and renew their minds. Let's just stay with the word! Prove all things and hold fast to that which is good.

Pray for kings and all that are in authority that we might live a quiet and peaceable life both inwardly and outwardly. This pleases God. Just agree with Him on this! It makes Him happy!

OK! Back to the text!

*1 Timothy 2:1-4 I exhort therefore, that, first of all, supplications, prayers, intercessions, and giving of thanks, be made **for all men**; For kings, and for all that are in authority; **that we** may lead a quiet and peaceable life in all godliness and honesty. For this is good and acceptable in the sight of God our Savior; **Who will have all men to be saved,** and to come unto the knowledge of the truth.*

We pray for kings – "so that *we*…"

Again, we pray for them for us.

And what is the purpose of it all? Why do we pray for the government? Why does God want us to enjoy a tranquil life inwardly and outwardly?

Because He wants all people "to be saved and to come to the knowledge of the truth!"

God wants all people to be saved and He has commissioned believers to preach the good news that saves. When the body of Christ is strong and blessed they'll reach out with joy and be a blessing to all families of the earth. They'll feed the poor, clothe the naked, support missionaries, build churches and print bibles! They'll take this wonderful gospel to the ends of the earth and make disciples of all nations. That's why we pray for the government!

You could paraphrase Paul's words like this. "Pray for the government so that the body of Christ will be blessed and enjoy favorable conditions to preach the gospel and reach the lost."

We pray for the government – for us – so that people will get saved. Indirectly, this makes even a prayer for the government a prayer for believers.

And by the way, we don't pray for the government to push our politics or to get "our man or our woman" in office. We don't always know everything that we think we know about politics. We don't always know who would be the right or wrong person for the job.

I know we think we do – but Jesus and the apostles did a pretty good job under a sick and perverse Roman government.

Not all "pro-life" and "traditional-marriage" candidates are godly people. Not all "pro-abortion" and "gay-marriage" candidates are wicked. In a sense, they're all bad – they're all sinners – even some who claim to be Christians. Claiming to be a Christian doesn't make you one and you almost have to claim to be a Christian to get elected in America.

We need to pray, trust God and spend less time, money and effort on trying to create a "theocracy" down here. That's not our commission! That's not what Jesus called us to do!

He said that His kingdom is not of this world!

Be informed, vote according to your conscience, be a prophetic voice to your community but please don't let your political party be your primary identity. First and foremost, you are an ambassador of Christ. The campaign platform of our Kingdom is good news, liberty, health and abundant life in Christ!

Many people who need Jesus are turned off by "Christian" party politics. I understand that they are often wrong but they are also lost. Walk in love. Be salt and light but be wise. No one has to be a member of our favorite political party to go to heaven.

Lastly, notice that Paul told Timothy to make "supplications, prayers, intercessions, and giving of thanks, **_for all men_**; for kings, and for all that are in authority."

"For all men" includes supplicating, praying and making

intercession – with thanksgiving – for the lost. Of course, we should be doing all of that but don't forget that Christians are included in "all men" or "all people" too! (Christians are still people in case you didn't know that.)

Some think we are extraterrestrials. We're not.

The New International Version translates "all men" as "everyone". The word in the Greek text is "anthropos" which literally means all people, both male and female. Christians are people and would by definition be included in the word "everyone" or "all men".

Although Paul doesn't specifically say in this scripture that praying for believers is priority number one, the principle can be clearly seen in other things he wrote.

*Galatians 6:10 Therefore, as we have opportunity, let us do good to all men, **especially** to those who are of the household of faith.*

Paul instructs us to "do good to all men". Once again "all men" simply refers to all people. *Praying* for them would be doing something good for them, wouldn't it?

Notice now, that he prioritizes which people should get our attention first. The word *"especially"* denotes priority.

We should use every opportunity to bless
"all people"
BUT
we should make it a priority
to bless those who are of the
"household of faith".

In other words, if you only have the time and resources to do one thing, do this one first.  Don't leave this one out. Bless all people but make sure your brothers and sisters are taken care of!

The NIV translates it like this:

*Galatians 6:10 Therefore, as we have opportunity, let us do good to all people, especially to those who belong to the family of believers.*

We're a family. We should love one another at least as much as we love our natural families. We're God's family! Jesus said, "Love one another as I have loved you."

Families stick together.
    Families fight for each other.
        Families support each other.
            Families take each other's needs seriously.

At least they should!

The Living Bible says it like this:

**Galatians 6:10** *That's why whenever we can we should always be kind to everyone, and especially to our Christian brothers.*

Our Christian brothers and sisters should be priority to us.

We need each other. We are joined together in faith. We have the same Father, the same Lord, the same Spirit and the same commission.

We also have the same enemy. We need to protect and defend each other!

Paul wrote this by the inspiration of the Holy Spirit. God wants us to put the body of Christ at the top of our "doing good" list.

We should do something good especially for our brothers and sisters in Christ. We should especially help the family of God.

Prayer is doing something good for people; it helps them, supports them, protects them and strengthens them. We should make it a priority to pray for the household of faith.

Remember, in the Old Testament God told Abraham, "I am going to bless you and make you a blessing." This is God's way of blessing all the families of the earth.

**He blesses us.**
**We bless them.**

Sadly, much of the body of Christ is not walking in the blessing that God has for them. Let's pray for them! Prayer can bring blessing to the body of Christ so that they will in turn be the blessing that God has called them to be!

Of course, we can and should pray for the lost, for the government, for Israel and for our own needs. But priority number one on our "prayer list" should be praying for one another.

Again, you may be thinking that praying for the lost is more important because their need is of eternal importance.

I understand that.

But even though the need of unbelievers is of eternal importance, praying for the body of Christ is more important. The eternal needs of the lost will only be met when the church reaches out with the blessings and power of God and His gracious offer of eternal life.

### When the church is blessed, the world will automatically be blessed!

One last tip from **1 Timothy 2:1-4.** When praying for international, national and local leaders, don't forget to pray that they would be saved. No matter which party affiliation they represent or what worldview they espouse, they are precious, eternal souls and God loves them.

Later I will share more reasons why praying for the body of Christ is so important but first let's look at some more PNO *(Priority Number One)* Scriptures.

# 3. JESUS THE INTERCESSOR

John chapter seventeen is often referred to as the great intercessory prayer of Jesus. Earlier in the evening on the night that He was betrayed and arrested, Jesus taught His disciples many important truths.

And then He prayed for them.

He prayed for believers.

Note the unusual statement He makes in this prayer:

*John 17:6-9* *I have manifested Your name to the men whom You have given Me out of the world. They were Yours, You gave them to Me, and they have kept Your word. 7 Now they have known that all things which You have given Me are from You. 8 For I have given to them the words which You have given Me; and they have received them, and have known surely that I came forth from You; and they have believed that You sent Me. 9* ***I pray for them. I do not pray for the world*** *but for those whom You have given Me, for they are Yours.*

Huh?

**"I do not pray for the world."**

What?

Wait a minute! I thought Jesus loved the world!

What's up with that?

If He loved the world, why didn't He pray for the world?

???

Did He or did He not love the world?

Yes, of course He did – AND He still loves the world. He just didn't pray for them.

He knew that praying for them wasn't what they needed most.
　　He knew that praying for them wasn't the biggest priority.
　　　　He knew that praying for them wouldn't fix their problem!

You know what else? There's not a single scripture anywhere in the New Testament that says that Jesus <u>ever</u> prayed for the lost.

Maybe He did.
Maybe He didn't.
We don't know.
The Bible doesn't say.

We do know that there is no record of Him ever praying for the lost.

Think of it! Jesus, who loves the world with all of His heart, said, "I do not pray for the world."

Why would He pray for His disciples – who were already believers – but not for the world? For the same exact reason we mentioned earlier!

*The lost do not get saved by our prayers but by believing the gospel.*

*1 Corinthians 1:21 For after that in the wisdom of God the world by wisdom knew not God, **it pleased God by the foolishness of preaching to save them that believe**.*

To believe it, they've got to hear it.
To hear it, someone's got to preach it.

*Romans 10:13-14 For "whoever calls on the name of the Lord shall be saved." 14 How then shall they call on Him in whom they have not believed? And how shall they believe in Him of whom they have not heard? And how shall they hear without a preacher?*

Jesus knew that He would be returning to the Father. He knew that the salvation of humanity would now – to a great degree – be in the hands of His disciples. He knew that if the lost were going to be saved, His disciples would have to give their lives to the preaching of the gospel!

Read the whole prayer in John chapter 17.

(Did you read it yet?)

Well – here's the summary:

He prayed that His disciples and those who come to believe the Gospel would be strengthened, sanctified, protected and unified. Believers need to be strengthened, sanctified, protected and unified to fulfill their most important purpose – reaching the lost.

Sadly, there's so much disunity and even a great lack of love for one another in the body of Christ.

Just look at YouTube, Facebook and other PUBLIC PLACES where Christians tear each other apart before the eyes and ears of a confused, deceived, lost and dying world. It's no wonder they think we're crazy!

Praying for the body of Christ will increase our love for the body of Christ.

I know this by experience!
    Been there, done that, bought the T-Shirt.
        It's a good one – one of my favorites!

I used to think it was my job to correct everyone's flakey doctrine. I was pretty arrogant about it and could wax eloquent in my pompous rhetoric. And then one day I found out that I wasn't the head of the body of Christ.

Jesus is.

Yes, sound doctrine is important. And yes again, there are times to confront and correct.

But some people think that God has called them to straighten everybody out! They imagine themselves to be heaven's infallible theology police or God's all-knowing inspectors of orthodoxy! Believing themselves to be the only reliable and flawless judges of sound doctrine, they rip people apart, tear people down and then condemn them to the eternal fires of hell. Their favorite words are "heretic", "false prophet" and "apostate". Anyone who disagrees with them or anyone with whom they disagree is denounced as if they were children of the devil!

Sorry to go on about this, but I believe it's necessary.

It's important to correct and confront doctrinal error but when we do, we should do it in the spirit of love. We should do it with patience, gentleness, meekness, humility and longsuffering.

The Bible says so – over and over!

But today we've got these
- HERESY HUNTERS –
self-righteous "know-it-alls"
who think it's their ministry to point out everyone's errors
- except their own -
and they make the whole body of Christ look like mean,
hateful, small hearted, unloving, narrow-minded,
baptized in prune juice creatures that no one
in their right mind wants anything to do with!

(Breathe Fred, breathe.)

Ok, I'm better now.

People who constantly criticize, condemn and berate others in the body of Christ are certainly not people who are praying for the body of Christ.

When we pray regularly for the body of Christ we will become generous, loving and big hearted. We will learn to thank God for one another despite our various theological differences.

YES, I KNOW THAT DOCTRINE IS IMPORTANT. (Don't get me started again.) ☺

Sound doctrine is very important but I believe that we should also follow the axiom coined by Marco Atonio de Dominis, "In necessariis unitas, in dubiis libertas, in omnibus caritas."

> **Unity in necessary things,**
> **Liberty in doubtful things,**
> **Charity (love) in all things.**

Unity does not necessarily mean unified doctrine in all theological matters. Unity is a matter of the heart and of love. Yes, the necessary doctrines required for salvation must be kept pure but many people are fighting and arguing before a lost and dying world about things that are not really necessary.

For example, imagine the following fictional Facebook thread:

> **TrueBeliever:** My pastor said that Christians who speak in tongues are not even real Christians. He went to a conference called "Weird Fire" and got the low-down.

> **JesusSaves:** What? Nonsense! Your pastor is so wrong, dude! Speaking in tongues is for all Christians! The Bible says so! It's a blessing! I thank my God that I speak in tongues more that you all! LOL!

> **TrueBeliever:** If you really believe that you're a heretic and going to hell! ☹

> **JesusSaves:** WOW! So sad! ☹ You don't even believe the Bible! Satan has deceived you and blinded you! Are you sure you're even saved?

> **TrueBeliever:** I'm not blind, you are! You're probably one of those health and wealth crazymatics!!!

> **JesusSaves:** Better well and blessed than sick and broke like you! You're just a Pharisee. So sad-you-see! ☺ LOL

> **Atheist:** Richard Dawkins was right about you people! You're all deluded! You can't even agree with each other about your made up daddy in the sky.

> **TrueBeliever:** @Atheist: Who cares what you and Dawkins say? The Bible says that atheists are fools and on their way to hell!

**JesusSaves:** @Atheist: That's right! We're not deluded, you're deluded, dude! People who believe in evil-ution are blind! Random selection never created anything – God did! Repent while you still have time!

**TrueBeliever:** @JesusSaves: Amen! At least we agree on something!

**Jesus Saves:** Praise the Lord, brother!

**True Believer:** Are you a "young earth" or an "old earth" creationist?

**Jesus Saves:** Old earth!

**True Believer:** I knew it! You are so going to hell!

**Atheist:** *Atheist has left the conversation.*

Yep. ☹

Admittedly, I invented that "Facebook" thread but you'll find things similar to that and MUCH WORSE on social media. Many Christians are tearing each other apart before a deceived and confused, lost and dying, suffering and sighing world that Jesus gave His life for!

What you believe about tongues, health and wealth, old earth or young earth creationism will not determine whether you or anyone else will go to heaven or not!

We need to major on the majors and not on the minors. We need to walk in love for the sake of Jesus and for the world outside our four walls!

But I digress.

Let me get back to the point.

Jesus prayed for His disciples.
He didn't pray for the world.

Let's read further in John 17:

*John 17:20 Neither pray I for these alone, but **for them also***

***which shall believe*** *on me through their word*

He did not pray for the world.
    He prayed for His disciples.
        He prayed for those who would believe in Him.
        He prayed for believers.

What the lost need is the gospel! If believers are strong, unified, sanctified and blessed they are going to reach out to the world with the gospel. But if they are weak, divided, carnal and defeated, we could pray for the world until we're blue in the face with little or no results.

Jesus told His disciples, "Go into all the world and *preach* the gospel to every creature." He didn't say, "Stay in the comfy, cozy church and *pray* for the lost." Just sayin'.

He *did* give instructions about how to pray *concerning* the lost. Let's read in Matthew's Gospel.

***Matthew 9:36*** *But when He saw the multitudes, He was moved with compassion for them, because they were weary and scattered, like sheep having no shepherd. 37 Then He said to His disciples, "The harvest truly is plentiful, but the laborers are few. 38 Therefore pray the Lord of the harvest to send out laborers into His harvest."*

He saw the multitudes.
    They were weary and scattered.
        He was moved with compassion.

He did not pray for them.

He did not tell the disciples to pray for them.

This is not a prayer for the lost.

This is a prayer "for the saints."

He told us to ask the Lord of the harvest to send laborers into His harvest. The harvest field of God is made up of the multitudes who are lost and scattered with no shepherd. The laborers are BELIEVERS who will preach the good news, heal the sick and set the captives free! This prayer is a prayer for believers.

It literally means to pray that the Father would
 thrust believers out,
   give them a kick in the backside,
     get them out of their comfort zones
       and send them to the highways and byways
         in search of the lost.

Someone once sang, "What the world needs now is love sweet love." But what the world really needs now is laborers.

The multitudes of weary and scattered lost sheep desperately need compassionate Christian workers who will bring them the good news. They need a laborer, a preacher, a teacher, a witness, a workmate, a school friend, a neighbor who will tell them about Jesus. They need our Shepherd.

They need YOU more than they need your prayers!

In the book of Acts we read a very similar prayer, prayed by the early church – you know – the apostolic church – the real-deal church! ☺

**Acts 4:29-30** *Now, Lord, look on their threats, and grant to Your servants that with all boldness they may speak Your word, 30 by stretching out Your hand to heal, and that signs and wonders may be done through the name of Your holy Servant Jesus."*

Grant boldness to whom?
To the lost?
NO!

Grant boldness to the servants of God; to believers!

They prayed for one another!

They prayed that they would be bold to preach in the Name of Jesus. They prayed that God would stretch out His hand to confirm the Gospel with healing and signs and wonders.

This world IS in great need and the body of Christ HAS what they need. That's one reason why praying for the body of Christ is priority number one in prayer.

Paraphrasing Paul in **Romans 10:13-14** he asks, "How can the lost call upon the Name of the Lord and be saved without a preacher?" He didn't ask, "How can they be saved without someone praying for them?"

Praying for the lost can open doors and soften hearts but if they never hear the Gospel they won't be saved.

Instead of prioritizing prayer for the lost, we should prioritize prayer for the body of Christ! We have been commissioned to reach the lost!

Maybe you're thinking,
    "What about my needs?
        What about my issues?
            I need prayer too!"

Boo-hoo! ☹ ☺

Just kidding. Yes, we all have needs and it is right and biblical to bring our requests to God.

Jesus said, *"Ask and it shall be given you." (Matt. 7:7)*

He told us to pray, *"Give us this day our daily bread." (Matt. 6:11)*

But He didn't say to beg and worry, or make our needs and issues the biggest priority in our lives. He simply said ask.

Ask in faith.
Give us this day our daily bread.
Trust God.

It's right to bring our requests to God but our personal needs shouldn't be our biggest priority. Wouldn't that be a bit selfish?

Just askin'.

In **Matthew 6:25-34** Jesus tells us not to worry about our material needs. God knows we need stuff. He takes care of the sparrows and the lilies of the fields. We are more important to him than birds and flowers! He'll take care of us if we trust Him.

Don't worry.

Did you just say, "Easier said than done"?

In **verse 33** Jesus tells us how to do this. He gives us the key to living a worry free life.

*Matthew 6:33 But seek first the kingdom of God and His righteousness, and all these things shall be added to you.*

If we'll do what He says right here, we won't have to spend much time talking to God about our personal needs.

Could it be that some of us who are always going on and on about our needs and issues are doing so because we are not following Jesus' instructions in **Matthew 6:33**?

Just askin'. Again.

Maybe if we did what Jesus said, we wouldn't have to try to "talk God into" meeting our needs.

Just sayin'.

(Am I getting on your nerves yet?)

Jesus said, "Seek first" – this denotes priority. Seek *first* the kingdom of God and His righteousness.

What does that even mean?
>What is God's kingdom?
>>How do we put God's kingdom first?

**Romans 14:17** tells us that the kingdom of God is not meat and drink but righteousness, joy and peace in the Holy Ghost!

(Nothing against eating and drinking – I am a fan of both – but that's not what the kingdom is.)

Righteousness, joy and peace are the spiritual qualities or characteristics of the kingdom of God. The very atmosphere of the kingdom is permeated with righteousness, joy and peace!

You can breathe deeply and relax! You'll find rest!

Taste and see that the Lord is good!

But what is the kingdom of God in a practical sense?

A kingdom consists of a king, his subjects and his domain. Jesus is our King and we are His subjects or the citizens of His kingdom.

Putting the kingdom of God first means putting God and His people first. One way that we can do this is by making God's family priority number one in our prayer life!

If we'll do that, God will certainly do what He promised. All the material things that we need for our lives and ministries will be added to us.

Listen to this wonderful promise of God.

*Philippians 4:6-7 Be anxious for nothing, but in everything by prayer and supplication, with thanksgiving, let your requests be made known to God; and the peace of God, which surpasses all understanding, will guard your hearts and minds through Christ Jesus.*

I would never make light of your personal challenges and problems. My heart breaks for the multitudes of my brothers and sisters who are suffering! I'm not trying to minimize the importance of their needs. There are so many who are suffering in sickness, poverty, bondage, oppression, depression, persecution and so on. Their needs is one of the reasons I am writing this book! I'm trying to enlist some prayer warriors to help!

I'm also trying to help us look beyond our *problems* to the *solution*.

I believe that if we follow God's instructions, we are going to reap a harvest of benefits. If we sow prayer, we will reap prayer. It's biblical.

*Galatians 6:7-8 Do not be deceived, God is not mocked; for whatever a man sows, that he will also reap. 8 For he who sows to his flesh will of the flesh reap corruption, but he who sows to the Spirit will of the Spirit reap everlasting life.*

If you need prayer, pray for someone else. Pray for their needs and God will raise up people to pray for your needs. Sowing prayer is one way to sow to the Spirit. If we do that we will reap life!

Maybe you feel weak right now. Maybe you think you don't have the strength to go on. But if you'll sow some prayer for your brothers and sisters in Christ, I am persuaded that God will strengthen you! I am persuaded that you will reap life and a harvest of people praying for you!

No matter what we need, God is concerned about it. We're not to worry about our needs but to ask and give thanks. If we'll spend more time giving thanks and less time worrying we will experience more peace and answered prayer.

Seek first the Kingdom.

Follow the Master.

Pray for believers.

Jesus did.

# 4. PAUL'S PRAYER LIFE

Let's look at some things that Paul wrote about his own prayer life. After all, he's the one who said that we should make it a priority to pray "for all saints".

He also told us to imitate him or follow him as he imitated and followed Christ.

**1 Corinthians 11:1** *Imitate me, just as I also imitate Christ.*

Paul knew Jesus well and was striving to imitate Him. It shouldn't be too big of a stretch to believe that we can learn something about how Jesus prays from Paul's prayer life.

And yes, Jesus still prays!
    He's seated at the right hand of God
        and He's still making intercession

        for believers!
        ☺

**Hebrews 7:25** *Therefore He is also able to save to the uttermost those who come to God through Him, since He always lives to make intercession for them.*

He is making intercession right now for you and for me and for all who have come to God through Him!

Aren't you glad? I sure am!

Since Paul was following Christ, he must have followed this aspect of His life as well, right? Paul had a very deep and intimate relationship with Jesus. He learned the Gospel by revelation of Jesus. He was tutored by Jesus Himself!

*Galatians 1:11-12 But I make known to you, brethren, that the gospel which was preached by me is not according to man. 12 For I neither received it from man, nor was I taught it, but it came through the revelation of Jesus Christ.*

From this we can conclude that his prayer life, as well as every other part of his life, was strongly influenced by Jesus. If you want to know how Jesus would pray today, look at Paul's prayer life and imitate it.

I am convinced that he learned about priority number one in prayer directly from Jesus. He had a very close and intimate relationship with Him. He was caught up into the third heaven.

*2 Corinthians 12:1-5 It is doubtless not profitable for me to boast. I will come to visions and revelations of the Lord: 2 I know a man in Christ who fourteen years ago — whether in the body I do not know, or whether out of the body I do not know, God knows — such a one was caught up to the third heaven. 3 And I know such a man — whether in the body or out of the body I do not know, God knows — 4 how he was caught up into Paradise and heard inexpressible words, which it is not lawful for a man to utter.*

He heard and saw things that no one else did. Maybe he even saw Jesus at the right hand of God praying for us! Maybe that's where he learned about the importance and the priority of praying for believers! Maybe.

We already read **Ephesians 6:18** and **Romans 8:26-27** where Paul specifically speaks of praying for the saints. But now let's see if he practiced what he preached. That'll be pretty easy to do since he begins nearly every one of his letters with a prayer.

*Romans 1:9 For God is my witness, whom I serve with my spirit in the gospel of his Son, that **without ceasing** I make mention of you **always** in my prayers.*

Always and without ceasing, Paul mentioned the believers in Rome in his prayers.

*1 Corinthians 1:4 I thank my God **always** on your behalf, for the grace of God which is given you by Jesus Christ;*

He thanked God always for the grace of God given to his Christian brothers and sisters in Corinth!

*Ephesians 1:15-16 Wherefore I also, after I heard of your faith in the Lord Jesus, and love unto all the saints, **cease not** to give thanks for you, making mention of you in my prayers;*

He never ceased to give thanks and mention the Christians in Ephesus in his prayers.

*Philippians 1:3-4 I thank my God upon **every remembrance** of you, **always** in **every** prayer of mine for you all making request **with joy**,*

Every time he thought about his dear brothers and sisters in Philippi, he thanked God and prayed for them. We should do this too!

There may be times when the Holy Spirit puts someone on our heart. These are special leadings and it's very important at these times to obey God and pray. Never ignore these urgent impressions! It could be the differences between life and death!

Other times, we are simply reminded of someone by some kind of coincidence. Maybe we see or hear something that reminds us of them. These are great opportunities to pray! Every remembrance means every remembrance.

For example, when I see a guy with a big nose, it immediately reminds me of the brother in our church with that amazing snout! (Is that your nose or are you eating a banana?) It's a great opportunity to pray for him. Another person in our church drives a bright yellow van. When I see a car or a van with that color it reminds me of them – and that's a reminder to pray for them!

Paul said he prayed for the believers in Philippi "upon every remembrance". We don't need a special leading to pray for believers. We might just be reminded of them by some coincidence. Let's bless them! Let's help them! Let's pray for them.

Paul did it with rejoicing! Apparently, it's fun!

**Colossians 1:3** *We* **give thanks** *to God and the Father of our Lord Jesus Christ, praying* **always** *for you*

He gave thanks and prayed always for the household of faith in Colossae! If we'd do this, it would immediately solve 95% of the problems in most churches! Instead of criticizing, complaining and fighting one another we should be giving thanks and praying for one another.

You can't criticize and berate someone when you are giving thanks for them.

Now I know the people in your church are not perfect – but neither are you!

Find something about them that you can thank God for. Once you start thanking God you'll be reminded of other things. Give thanks and pray for your church and for the whole body of Christ.

**Colossians 1:9a** *For this cause we also, since the day we heard it,* **do not cease** *to pray for you*

This is still the first chapter of Colossians and Paul is already telling them a second time that he's praying for them. "I never cease to pray for you."

He was inspired of the Holy Spirit to tell them that he was praying for them!

It helps people to know that you are praying for them. Tell your pastors that you're praying for them. Tell your church family that you're praying for them. It'll help them.

And then make sure that you really do pray for them.

**1 Thessalonians 1:2** *We* **give thanks** *to God* **always** *for you all, making mention of you in our prayers;*

Always thanking God for them. Always praying for them.

Are you getting the point?

**1 Thessalonians 3:9-10** *For what thanks can we render to God* *again for you, for all the joy wherewith we joy for your sakes before our God; **Night and day** praying exceedingly that we might see your face, and might perfect that which is lacking in your faith?*

Just to make it clear, he didn't just pray for them in the morning. He didn't just pray for them in the afternoon. He didn't just pray for them in the evening. He prayed for them night AND day. Both night and day are good times to pray. Hey! That rhymes! Night and day are good times to pray – for believers!

**2 Thessalonians 1:11a** *Wherefore also **we pray always** for you.*

Here Paul writes, "*We* always pray for you". Note the "we".

This means that Paul didn't just pray for them in his own personal prayer times with the Lord. He also prayed for them with his prayer group. He enlisted others to help him pray for the believers in Thessalonica! Paul, Timothy and Silvanus came together and said, "We need to pray for our friends in Christ at Thessalonica."

Do you have a prayer group? Get them to pray with you for the body of Christ!

**2 Timothy 1:3** *I thank God, whom I serve from my forefathers with pure conscience, that **without ceasing** I have remembrance of thee in my prayers **night and day**;*

Without ceasing.
Night and day.
Again.

**Philemon 1:4** *I thank my God, making mention of you **always** in my prayers,*

We've already seen that Paul always prayed for the churches but here we see him always praying for an individual brother as well. Let's not pray superficially or only in a general way.

"Dear God,
bless all the Christians
in the whole wide world.
Amen."

No – let's get specific. If you know of a brother or sister in need of help, pray specifically for them. If you know specifically what they need, tell God about it. Ask the Holy Spirit to help you pray. Ask Him if there's anyone that He'd like you to pray for. Ask Him if there's anything specific you should be asking.

If you are open to His leading, He will show you things. Prayer is a joint effort. We are praying and He is helping us! He helps us help others and together we are stronger!

Paul prayed,
>  gave thanks,
>>  without ceasing,
>>>  upon every remembrance,
>>>>  night and day,
>>>>>  and always

for the believers in Rome, Corinth, Ephesus, Colossae, Philippi and Thessalonica.

He prayed for Timothy and Philemon
>  and others,
>>  without ceasing,
>>>  night and day
>>>>  and always.

Apparently Paul spent **A LOT OF TIME** in prayer for believers. I don't believe he was exaggerating! (The Holy Spirit didn't inspire Paul to exaggerate. I mean, after all this is scripture!)

Yes, Paul prayed for Israel. He also prayed for the government. But praying for "all the saints" was most definitely Paul's number one priority in prayer. This is why he adamantly encouraged us – by inspiration of the Holy Spirit – to pray for one another – to pray for all the saints.

There is also a wealth of information about how he prayed for believers. This is a tremendous help to us. The prayers contained within his letters are inspired of the Holy Spirit.

They are prayers we can learn from.

They are prayers addressing the greatest needs in the body of Christ.

They are prayers that we can memorize and pray for our fellow believers.

We'll take a closer look at those prayers in a moment, but before we do, let's look at a few more "PNO" scriptures.

# 5. INDIRECT REFERENCES

***Acts 4:29-30*** *Now, Lord, look on their threats, and **grant to Your servants** that with all boldness they may speak Your word,*

When I first saw "priority number one in prayer" I was amazed that I hadn't seen it earlier. It's all throughout the New Testament. Time and time again we are encouraged to pray for one another. We've already looked at some of those scriptures. But there are a number of other passages where the principle – though not directly stated – is implied.

For example, Peter and John had been threatened by the Jewish Sanhedrin. They were arrested and commanded to stop teaching in the Name of Jesus. After they were released, they went to their "own company" and prayed.

It's so good and important to be part of a local fellowship. It's so vital to have brothers and sisters that you can count on to pray for you and to pray with you *There is exponential power in united prayer!*

Peter and John told their church family what the High Priest, elders, rulers and scribes had commanded them. When they heard the report they "lifted up their voices to God in one accord" and prayed.

How did they pray?

They began by praising God.
    Then they proclaimed their faith in His ability.

Then they told God about the threat.
Then they asked God for boldness to preach
and for supernatural help.

It was a pretty simple prayer. With all the threats to our faith today, we could and should pray this prayer verbatim for all of our churches all of the time.

However, it's also important to note what they *didn't* pray about.

They had just experienced problems with supreme council or government of the Jews. However, they didn't pray for them. They didn't ask God to remove them and replace them with new rulers who would support their efforts. They didn't ask God to raise up a new Christian Party who could possibly win the next election. They didn't pray for the government in this story at all.

Of course it's good to pray for the government.
They need it!
They need it BIG time!
We pray for them for us!

However, they didn't do that here.

They also didn't enter into spiritual warfare and fight against the hosts of demonic religious spirits that were trying to hinder their ministry. We don't read of any binding or loosing, commanding or demanding, pulling down, casting out, breaking the power of or releasing the power of anything or anyone.

No mention of it.

Don't get me wrong, I believe that there is a place in prayer for exercising authority against wicked spirits but they didn't do that here. And not only that, we could shout at the devil all day long but if we don't go and tell people about Jesus, the enemy will still have every right in the world to stay in town and mess up people's lives.

If you want to change the "spiritual atmosphere" of your city, get people born again and make disciples of them. Each new convert changes the "spiritual atmosphere" a little more and increases the influence of the Kingdom of God in your town!

Another thing that they didn't pray for was for protection. Think about it! They were being persecuted but they didn't think to pray for protection.

> They didn't pray for the government.
> They didn't bind or loose.
> They didn't pray for protection.

Nothing against those things, I just wanted to point out that they didn't pray like that here.

But their prayer was powerful!

God was so pleased with their prayer that He shook the whole place where they had gathered. It was as if God heard their prayer and said,

## "YES!!! I LIKE THAT KIND OF PRAYING!"

For whom did they pray? Let's look again.

*Acts 4:29-30 Now, Lord, look on their threats, and **grant to Your servants** that with all boldness they may speak Your word, 30 by stretching out Your hand to heal, and that signs and wonders may be done through the name of Your holy Servant Jesus."*

They prayed for the servants of God.
> They prayed for each other.
> > They prayed for the saints.

It was priority number one in this case.
It was more important than praying for the government.
It was more important than "binding" evil spirits and so on!
It's more important than praying for protection!

From this prayer we learn how to pray when faced with persecution.

Pray for boldness. Pray for power. Some of our brothers and sisters are facing serious persecution right now. What they need more than anything is boldness to continue in the faith and to speak the word of God. They need His power to be witnesses!

In the western world we don't have to deal with much persecution, but we do face threats and those threats are growing!

Political correctness,
      blatant attacks against Christian values;
         institutionalized immorality,
           and the war to limit freedom of speech,
             freedom of conscience
              and freedom of religion
                are driving some believers
                  into the closet.

They are fearful and hiding behind the four walls of their churches!
(If they even go to church at all!)

It is so important to pray for boldness for the body of Christ!

From this prayer, we also learn that it is biblical to pray for the power of God and the gifts of the Spirit. We can pray that our churches and our fellow believers would have the supernatural equipment needed to preach the gospel. Praying for the gifts of the Holy Spirit is in order! The apostles and those who gathered to pray asked God for the power gifts of the Spirit.

The power gifts are:
The gifts of healings,
the working of miracles
and the gift of special faith!
(Read **1 Corinthians 12:7-11**)

Pray for a greater manifestation of these gifts in the body of Christ. If we ever needed God's supernatural power to confirm His word, it is now. There are so many voices in the world – so many religions, so many causes, so many special interests, so many lobbies and so many advocates for the devil.

We need God's healing and miracle working power more than ever. Pray this Acts chapter 4 prayer for your church and for the whole body of Christ.

Another PNO scripture is found in Colossians 4.

**Colossians 4:12** *Epaphras, who is one of you, a bondservant of Christ, greets you, always laboring fervently for you in prayers, that you may stand perfect and complete in all the will of God.*

Epaphras was praying for his church family in Colossae. From him we learn that prayer can be work. It will never come natural to your flesh. There will always be resistance when you want to pray.

The enemy, the flesh and the un-renewed mind will try to keep us from prayer. There will be things that we have to overcome to become consistent in prayer.

It seems like every time I kneel to pray, ten thousand other thoughts try to get my attention!

"Don't you want to read the news first? Then you can pray more effectively for the world!"

"Don't you want to eat something first? Then you will be stronger and have more endurance."

"Don't you want to make that telephone call,
          send that e-mail,
                    check your Facebook page,
                              upload that important photo,
                                        write a blog article
                                                  or take a short nap?
                                                            Just a short one?"

It's kind of sad that people come in droves to the special "food events" at church but stay home in droves when there's a prayer meeting!

Church Picnic
Potluck Dinner
Church barbeque
Sweethearts banquet
Dinner on the grounds
Women's breakfast
Christmas banquet
Men's breakfast
Bake sale
Etcetera!
Buuuurp!
Excuse me!

Eatin's easy!
Prayer's work!

To be consistent in prayer requires discipline. I probably wouldn't have been at early morning prayer every day if I hadn't said it publicly. I'm just being honest! I was forced to either be there or be guilty of lying. I'm so glad that I had committed myself and made myself accountable!

Maybe it's time for more of us to make ourselves accountable. Genuine help, strength and freedom come when we are accountable to one another.

Epaphras labored fervently in prayer. If your prayer is lukewarm it won't get God's attention. If it doesn't mean much to you it won't mean much to Him. But when your prayer is a fervent desire and you pour out your heart to God, nothing can withstand its power!

*James 5:16b The prayer of a righteous man is powerful and effective. (NIV)*

Epaphras prayed that the church would stand perfect and complete in all the will of God. You can pray for your brothers and sisters in Christ that they would have the power to stand!

We all know people who started out doing the will of God and then gave up and quit. This is a prayer that will help them keep on keeping on! This prayer will give them strength to not only KNOW the word of God but to also DO the word of God.

Is it possible to stand perfect and complete in all the will of God?

It must be! The Holy Spirit inspired Paul to include this prayer in his letter to the Colossians!

Paul must have believed it was possible.

**All things are possible with God!**
**All things are possible to those who believe!**

If your brothers and sisters in Christ don't succeed to the full degree after your first prayer, don't give up! Keep supporting and strengthening them by praying again and again for them!

Prayer strengthens people.

Guess how I know that!

I've had times when I was so tired or discouraged that I didn't know how I was going to make it through the day. And then suddenly – without me doing anything special at all – a strength came upon me that was not my own. The burden lifted and my hope was restored. In that moment I knew that someone had been praying for me.

Oh, how thankful I am for the prayers of my family in Christ!!!

Speaking of being thankful:

*1 Corinthians 1:4 I thank my God always concerning you for the grace of God which was given to you by Christ Jesus,*

Paul thanked God for the grace that was given to the Corinthians! Grace gives us the power we need to stand strong. We can't stand perfect and complete in all the will of God without His grace.

I said it earlier but I am persuaded that if we would thank God for one another more often, we would have a lot fewer church splits, doctrinal wars and roasted pastors.

Instead of criticizing, give thanks.
Instead of complaining, give thanks.
Instead of gossiping, give thanks!

Maybe you feel as if your church is like the Corinthian church – carnal, immature, divided, immoral and flakey!

Thank God for them! Their immature and carnal behavior must make you look and feel like a spiritual giant! ☺

They might be weak and carnal now, but God's grace will make a difference in their lives! Thank God that His grace is working in them and through them. His grace is sufficient. His grace is made perfect in our weakness. Paul told Timothy, "Be strong in the grace that is in Christ Jesus!" (**2 Timothy 2:1**)

James said, "God gives more grace!" (**James 4:6**)

Give thanks for them and ask God to give your church family more grace to stand strong and do His will!

If we'll thank God for them, God will increase our love for them. If we really love them, they will know it. They will sense it and be open for our advice.

If we just want to tell everyone off, no one will be interested in what we have to say – even if what we have to say is right!

Paul spoke some very strong corrective words to the Corinthians but they recognized that it came from a heart of love. He had earned the right to speak into their lives. He founded that church. He was a spiritual father to them. They knew that his rebukes and admonishments were coming from a heart that was genuinely concerned about them. He didn't just berate them.

He loved them,
      prayed for them
           gave thanks for them!

*Then* he rebuked them and they repented.

Paul knew they were carnal, but he also knew that God's grace was still working in their lives. He knew that they were born again and wanted to serve God. He knew they were excited about Jesus and the power of God. He thanked God for it!

Think about the good things in people and not just the bad.

As I began to pray daily for the body of Christ, my love for the whole body of Christ increased! Instead of criticizing those who I didn't agree with, I began to thank God for the good things they were doing. I began to thank God for His grace in their lives.

Within a short time I developed a greater appreciation and a greater love for those in other churches and denominations. Some of them don't agree with everything that I believe but that doesn't change my love and appreciation for them. I don't necessarily agree with everything they teach or believe either but I love them!

They are my brothers and sisters in Christ! They are my family!

Are they perfect? No.
Am I? No.
Are you? No.

Never forget this; you can choose your friends but you can't choose your family.

Everyone who is born again is a member of our family regardless of which church or denomination they belong to. We may not agree with every point of their doctrine but if they are in Christ then they are also in us.

Remember?

**John 14:20** At that day ye shall know that I am in my Father, and ye in me, and I in you.

> I'm in Him, He's in me, He's in you.
> I'm in Him in you.
> You're in Him in me.

If I talk bad about you, I am talking bad about me. If I hurt you, I am hurting me. The Church has been working against herself way too much!

The devil loves division because it weakens God's family and makes them ineffective. (We'll look further at the subject of unity later on.)

But first let see what James says about praying for one another.

# 6. THAT YOU MAY BE HEALED

Another PNO verse is found in James 5.

***James 5:16*** *Confess your trespasses to one another, and pray for one another, that you may be healed. The effective, fervent prayer of a righteous man avails much.*

"Confess your trespasses". Before we dig any deeper into this verse maybe we should stop and confess our sins. ☺

Seriously. ☺

Maybe we haven't been praying for our pastors, our brothers and sisters, our churches, and the Body of Christ in general as much as we should have.

Maybe that's one of the reasons why some churches are weak and ineffective. It might even explain why some Christian leaders have fallen and scandals have happened. Truth be told, it could be that this is why so many churches are losing members and closing while militant atheists and new age gurus seem to be attracting larger followings. And perhaps this is why the fabric of Christian values, which was once the bedrock of our nation, has been torn to shreds before our very eyes.

Maybe.
Might be.
Could be.
Perhaps.

Of course there are other factors as well, but I am persuaded that we haven't been helping and supporting each other the way that we need to – the way we are called to – the way the Bible says we should.

Ok then.

When James speaks of confessing our sins to one another, there are three things that he doesn't mean.

He doesn't mean that we have to go to a priest to get God's forgiveness. Jesus is the one mediator between God and man.

He doesn't mean that we have to publicly confess our sins in a church service.

He also doesn't mean that we should boast about how bad we were before we got saved.

*A little side note:* Don't make your testimony juicier than it was. Don't refer to your B.C. life as if it were glamourous. Don't talk romantically about the fish, cucumbers, melons, leeks, onions and garlic. **(see Numbers 11:5)** And whatever you do, don't make it sound like those were the best days of your life.

They weren't.

James is simply saying that if you've hurt or offended someone, you need to fix it. There are many Christians who are offended and bitter because this verse has not been acted upon. Go tell them you are sorry. Ask for forgiveness. Get it right!

Maybe you are the one who is offended and you just said, "Amen".

Well, perhaps you should confess your sin of holding a grudge!

Moving on…

In **James 5:16**, God instructs us again to pray for one another. This time He tells us to pray for one another that we may be healed.

Do you know anyone who is sick in your church? They need your prayers. God said you should pray for them. The instruction is simple. Pray that they may be healed. This command reveals that

God wants to heal His children.

He wouldn't tell us to pray for something that He is not willing to do. In other words, if He doesn't want to do it, He wouldn't tell us to pray that He would!

That would be a mean thing to do.

God is not mean.

Imagine that I told my son that he could ask me to help him with his homework. The next day he comes home from school and says, "Dad, can you help me with my math homework?" I say, "No way! I don't want to help you with your homework! I'm playing Nintendo!" Then he reminds me, "But Dad, you said I could ask you to help me!" I answer, "I said you could *ask* – but I didn't say that I'd actually *help*!"

What would you think of me if I did that?

Of course, I wouldn't do that but if I did, you would think that I'm a pretty bad dad. And I would be. You would think that I'm a father who makes promises he's not willing to keep.

Many people think that God is a bad dad.
But He's not.

He said that we should pray for one another to be healed. Why? Because it is His desire – as our loving heavenly Father – to heal us and make us whole!

James didn't say, "Pray that they will be able to suffer with dignity." He didn't say, "Pray that this sickness will draw them closer to God." He didn't say, "Pray that they will learn whatever lesson God is trying to teach them through this sickness."

He didn't say any of that stuff!
He simply says, "Pray that they may be healed."

It is God's revealed will to heal us.

Apparently there can be a connection between the confession of sins and healing. Sometimes people might have to get some things straightened out in relationships before they are in position to receive healing.

They might have to apologize and ask for forgiveness. Or maybe they're the one who needs to forgive and let go of some things.

But that doesn't change the fact that God wants to heal them.

And just so that no one get's the wrong idea here – there are many different causes for sickness and disease. I'm not implying that everyone who's sick is sick because of a specific sin that they committed.

The causes of sickness could be spiritual, soulical or physical. Worry, stress, over-working, bitterness, jealousy, germs, smoking, over-eating, fear, condemnation, anger, hatred, greed, unbelief, sorrow, wrong thinking, an inferiority complex and so on can all be causes of sickness. The "so on" means that there are many other reasons and causes for sickness.

But regardless of the cause, James makes it clear that it is the will of God to heal His children.

We could say a lot more about it but that's a subject for a different book. The focus of this book is praying for one another. Pray that they may be healed.

Don't get nervous.
    Don't get weird.
        It's not your job to heal them.
            It's your job to pray for them.

I remember one of the first times I prayed for someone to be healed. I was very young in the Lord. I didn't know that much. I wasn't that wise. I was still simple enough to believe what the Bible says and to act upon it. (We should never lose that kind of simplicity.)

Anyway, a friend had water on the knee. His knee was swollen and in pain. I said to him, "Jesus said that believers will lay hands on the sick in His Name and they'll be healed. Do you want me to pray for you?" He asked, "Did Jesus really say that?" I said, "Yes" and then showed him Mark 16:17-18.

***Mark 16:17-18*** *And these signs will follow those who believe: In*

*My name they will cast out demons; they will speak with new
tongues; 18 they will take up serpents; and if they drink anything
deadly, it will by no means hurt them; they will lay hands on the
sick, and they will recover."*

After we read it, he said, "Then go ahead and lay your hand on my
knee". I did and I was almost as amazed as him that the swelling
went down and the pain left immediately.

My friend wasn't healed because I'm so special! Jesus said that
this is something all believers should do. I was just simple enough
to act upon it and it worked!

Sometimes I think that God is just waiting for someone to believe
His word enough to act upon it. Miracles happen when we believe
and act upon God's word!

John Wesley is quoted as saying, "God does nothing except in
response to believing prayer." Amen! Our God is a prayer
answering God!

There are many other things that we can pray about for the body
of Christ as well.

We can pray for married couples to walk in the love of God and be
good examples of Jesus' love for the church. We can pray that
they will have the wisdom, faith and courage to obey God's
instructions for marriage. We can pray that grace and peace
would fill their homes and marriages!

We can pray that Christian parents would have the wisdom
necessary to raise their children for Jesus in a world that is trying
to lead them away from Him.

We can pray that Christian singles would walk in a way that is
worthy of God and be happy and whole as a single until they find
the right mate – if they want to find a mate at all. Not all do. And
that's ok. They're like Paul in that sense.

We can pray that Christian employees would be good witnesses
for Jesus. Pray that they would have favor with their company and
be chosen for promotions and pay raises.

We can pray that Christian businessmen and women would have

favor and wisdom with banks, customers and politicians. We can pray that they would receive wisdom from God to make decisions that lead to success. We can pray that they would receive creative ideas that will bless humanity and earn millions! We can pray that they would be market leaders in their fields of business. We can pray that they would have the grace, integrity and courage to do the right things in a world where ethics and morals have been perverted or discarded altogether.

And we can pray for our church leaders. (We'll cover that more thoroughly in another chapter.)

Let's pray for one another that we might be healed. Let's pray for all the various needs in our family!

Speaking of needs – there are many – but one of them is more important than all the rest. If this need is met many other needs will automatically fall in line! What is the most important need in the body of Christ?

Read on.

# 7. THE NUMBER ONE NEED

Up until this point we have looked at 25 Scriptures that specifically refer to praying for believers. There are many others that we'll look at before we're done. But the evidence is starting to pile up that priority number one in prayer is praying for the body of Christ.

There are only three scriptures in the New Testament that even mention praying for the lost. We've already looked at two of them.

**Romans 10:1** *Brethren, my heart's desire and prayer to God for Israel is that they may be saved.*

Yes, it is right to pray for Israel and for others to be saved.

**1 Timothy 2:1-2** *Therefore I exhort first of all that supplications, prayers, intercessions, and giving of thanks be made for all men,*

Yes, praying for "all men" or "all people" would include praying for those who don't know Jesus yet. And yes, it's very important! But again, when we are doing good unto "all people" we should especially – as priority – do good to our family in Christ.

The third scripture, which speaks of praying for unbelievers is:

**Matthew 5:44** *But I say to you, love your enemies, bless those who curse you, do good to those who hate you, and pray for those who spitefully use you and persecute you,*

(Of course this could also be a prayer for certain folks in the body of Christ. Ahem… ☺ )

We are to pray for our unbelieving enemies, for all men and for Israel that they might be saved. It is good and right to pray that they would be saved. Even though the New Testament doesn't really tell us how to pray for them, it gives us principles that we can follow to pray effectively for them. I cover that subject more thoroughly in my book, "You and Your Whole House". Suffice it for now to say that praying for unbelievers opens the door for God to work in their lives.

When we pray for them, He can convict them of sin, righteousness and judgment.

We can break the power of the enemy over their lives.
We can ask God to reveal Jesus to them.
We can ask God to send laborers to them.
We can ask God to send angels to protect them and schedule divine appointments with His harvest workers, etc.

We should pray for unbelieving Jews and unbelieving Gentiles. We should pray for Muslims and Hindus. We should pray for Buddhists, Confucianists, Animists, Pantheists, Spiritists, Atheists and all the other -ists.

Yes, it's important to pray for the lost.

But it's even more important to pray for those who are called to *reach* the lost. Praying "for all the saints" is priority number one!

I'm repeating myself.
Intentionally.

In the last chapter we mentioned a number of things that we can pray about for believers but there is one specific need that is more urgent and important than the rest.

BECAUSE IT'S THE MOST IMPORTANT NEED, YOU SHOULD WRITE THIS ONE IN "ALL CAPS" ON YOUR PRAYER LIST.

Many think that praying for revival, unity or a fresh outpouring of the Holy Spirit is at the top of the list. Why wouldn't they? These are the things that are emphasized at nearly every major prayer gathering today. But they are not the things that Paul or any of the other Apostles put at the top of their prayer lists.

Others might think that praying for marriages and families is the greatest need because of the attack on the family. Some studies have shown that the divorce rate among Christians mirrors that of the world. This is a sad reality and reveals the great need to pray for Christian marriages and families. But there is a need even greater than that.

I'm not saying that we shouldn't pray for these things. We should. I'm just saying that these are not the things that the apostles emphasized when they prayed for the church.

I believe that if we pray biblically we will get biblical results. God gave us Holy Spirit inspired prayers to guide us in our prayer lives. It stands to reason that if we follow His instructions we will be more effective.

If we were to make a list of all the needs and problems in the body of Christ it would be a long list. Scientists have estimated that if a list like that were actually made, it would reach to the moon and back 7.3 times. (Not really – I just made that up.) But it *would be* a very long list!

Many of these very real needs and very serious problems however, are merely symptoms of the greatest need. If we can cure the disease, the symptoms will disappear. If we can pluck up the root, we won't have to deal with the fruit.

What is the most urgent need of the body of Christ? What can produce revival, unity and genuine Spirit-filled living? What can heal marriages and strengthen families?

(Drum roll please…)

## REVELATION KNOWLEDGE!

God's people are being destroyed because of lack of knowledge – revelation knowledge.

*Hosea 4:6 My people are destroyed for lack of knowledge. Because you have rejected knowledge, I also will reject you from being priest for Me; Because you have forgotten the law of your God, I also will forget your children.*

What we don't know can hurt us! A lack of knowledge opens the door to destruction in so many ways. According to Hosea, there are three possible causes of this lack.

Some people have never heard the truth.
> Others have heard the truth and rejected it.
>> Others have heard the truth and forgotten it.

Whatever the root cause may be, if we don't know what God wants us to know we will be at a disadvantage in life!

Revival, unity and Spirit-filled living are directly connected to knowing what God has already provided for us in Christ.

Strong marriages and families are built upon the revelation of what God said concerning marriage and family. They are built upon the revelation of His love for us and His love in us.

Abundant, victorious living is the result of knowing and acting upon redemptive truth.

Multitudes of Christians have very little knowledge about what God has done for them in Christ. Most of them know that God has forgiven their sins and will receive them into heaven one day but that is the extent of their knowledge of redemption. Forgiveness and the comfort of knowing that we are going to heaven are wonderful truths but there is so much more that Jesus provided for us in redemption.

There are promises, truths and wisdom for every area of our lives in the "here and now" as well as the hereafter. There is a victorious life waiting for every believer to experience. God has already given us everything that we need for life and godliness in Christ. But we need to KNOW these things. We need revelation.

*2 Peter 1:3-4 According as his divine power hath given unto us **all things** that pertain unto life and godliness, **through the knowledge of him that hath called us to glory and virtue**: Whereby are given unto us exceeding great and precious promises: that by these ye might be partakers of the divine nature, having escaped the corruption that is in the world through lust.*

Knowing Him and His promises will make us partakers of the divine nature. This revelation will enable us to walk above the lusts that are in this world. Instead of being slaves to fleshly bad habits we will see and realize that sin cannot dominate us. We will walk in a greater dimension of the victory that Jesus purchased for us on the cross!

**Romans 6:14** *For sin shall not have dominion over you, for you are not under law but under grace.*

Instead of worrying about lack we will live in the conscious reality that God always supplies all of our needs in Christ.

**Philippians 4:19** *And my God shall supply all your need according to His riches in glory by Christ Jesus.*

Instead of being intimidated by sickness and disease, we will see that Jesus healed us 2000 years ago when He gave His life for us.

**1 Peter 2:24** *who Himself bore our sins in His own body on the tree, that we, having died to sins, might live for righteousness — by whose stripes you were healed.*

Instead of trying to find someone to deliver us from demonic influences we will know that we have already been delivered. We will walk in the power and authority of the Name of Jesus!

**Colossians 1:13** *He has delivered us from the power of darkness and conveyed us into the kingdom of the Son of His love*

When I speak of knowing, seeing, realizing and being conscious of these truths I am speaking of revelation knowledge.

Many Christians are trying to talk God into giving them what he already gave them 2000 years ago! They are living like beggars when all the while they are kings.

There is a huge difference between information and revelation.

John Wesley spoke of the difference between mental agreement and believing with the heart. Many years of his life were spent mentally agreeing with God's word but there came a time when it became real to his heart and he was born again. This is what differentiates information from revelation.

It's not enough to have books and sermon notes on redemptive truth. Redemptive truth has to be a living reality within our hearts.

We must *know* it and not just be informed about it.

Think about a covered painting on an easel. Someone could describe what the painting looked like. They could tell you the subject matter, color scheme and media used to create it. But when the veil is pulled away, you get revelation! Suddenly you see details, nuances and hues that you had no way of knowing even existed! Revelation is like pulling the veil off the truth.

It is seeing behind the curtains. Now you know how all those amazing things work. Now you can put them to work yourself!

Revelation is like turning a light switch on. If you're married and ever had to get up in the middle of the night you'll understand this one. You don't want to wake your wife or husband so you quietly get out of bed and blindly try to navigate your way through the dark. Then you stub your big toe and try to hold back the "ouch".

If you had only turned on the light, you wouldn't have stubbed your toe. Too many Christians are stubbing their toes. They're walking with the lights off and not seeing everything clearly.

*John 8:31-32* *Then Jesus said to those Jews who believed Him, "If you abide in My word, you are My disciples indeed. 32 And you shall know the truth, and the truth shall make you free."*

Jesus said this to Jews who believed on Him. They were believers but not yet disciples. It's possible to be a believer and not be a disciple. Continuing in the word transforms a believer into a disciple.

Which are you?

My New King James Bible has a heading above this scripture that says, "The Truth Shall Make You Free". But that heading is not entirely true! Jesus didn't just say that the truth would make you free. He said "You will *know* the truth and the truth shall make you free."

It's only the truth that we *know* that has the power to make us free. When you really KNOW the truth it will change your life. It will change how you think, how you believe, how you talk and eventually how you live! "Knowing" in this sense refers to more than mere information. It refers to revelation.

**You don't really know a truth
unless it has made you free.
If it hasn't changed you,
it's not revelation to you!**

Imagine a heavyweight boxer who's preparing for an upcoming fight. He works out hard and trains every day. He also spends time studying his opponent. He finds out that his rival is 6' 2" and weighs 240 pounds. He looks at his pictures and it seems like he's chiseled out of solid rock - just solid muscle. He reads about how many fights he's won and lost. He watches videos from his opponent's last fights and sees that this dude has a wicked left hook.

That's information.

But on the day of the fight they're bobbing and weaving and in the second round that wicked left hook get's through and collides with his chin.

That's revelation.

The truth hit him like a ton of bricks!

It's nearly impossible to explain the difference between information and revelation. I remember going to Bible School and coming home after class with a heart full of revelation knowledge. I was so excited about these things and wanted to pass them on to my wife. I told her about the things I had learned and even used the same illustrations. And she'd be like, "Yeah, I know. I've heard that. That's right."

I could tell she wasn't seeing it like I was. When I was in class, the teacher was teaching by the anointing of the Holy Spirit and revelation was flowing to my heart. I went home and passed on the information – with apparently no anointing – ☹ – and it didn't have the same impact.

It is impossible for one human being to convey truth to another human being without the anointing. We need the Holy Spirit. We need the Spirit of wisdom and revelation!

Revelation is when the truth dawns on your heart. It's like reading a scripture 50 times and then all of a sudden YOU SEE something you never saw before.

It's that "Aha" moment! "Aha! I see it!"

Revelation is seeing a truth with your spirit. It is "knowing that you know that you know".

Revelation knowledge is the basis for strong faith.
    It will make you confident, fearless and bold.
        You will walk in a greater dimension of authority.

When revelation comes, doubt, insecurity and questioning will disappear. Overcoming faith takes their place and the believer becomes a master in life.

There are truths that are beyond the ability of our mental faculties to grasp.

There is a joy that's unspeakable and full of glory. You can't find words to express it but it's real!

There is a peace that passes understanding. Defying all logic this peace fills your heart and keeps your mind even in the middle of a crisis!

There is a love so high, so deep, so long and so wide – a love that passes all knowledge. You can't know it with your head, you can only know it with your heart!

It is impossible to find words better than the words the Bible uses to describe these things. But words alone cannot completely convey truth!

Words are powerful but they are limited. They can't express everything we need to know. There is a heart knowledge that transforms information into confidence, power and authority.

We need that.

Without revelation knowledge, believers will remain ignorant of their rights and privileges in Christ and live pretty much like ordinary people.

They will remain subject to the ups and downs of human existence instead of ruling and reigning in life with Christ as they are called to do. This is why there are numerous prayers in the New Testament letters concerning revelation knowledge.

When we really know what God did for us in Christ, it will end all the striving against each other in the body of Christ. He has already made us one with Himself and one with each other.

**1 Corinthians 6:17** *But he who is joined to the Lord is one spirit with Him.*

Praying for unity is important but it must be based upon the revelation that we are already one in Christ! Actually it is no longer necessary to pray, "Lord make us one." Jesus prayed that in the garden and the Father already answered that prayer!

We are one Spirit with the Lord. I'm in Him in you! We are already one! If we fight against each other, we are fighting against ourselves. If we talk poorly of one another, we're talking poorly of ourselves.

Paul wrote:

**Ephesians 4:1-3** *I, therefore, the prisoner of the Lord, beseech you to walk worthy of the calling with which you were called, 2 with all lowliness and gentleness, with longsuffering, bearing with one another in love, 3 endeavoring to keep the unity of the Spirit in the bond of peace.*

Note the words, "Endeavor to keep the unity of the Spirit." We can't endeavor to keep what we don't have.

We are already one but we have to bear with one another in love. We have to endeavor – try hard – to work at keeping the unity we already have!

I've gotta put up with you
And you've gotta put up with me.
I know I've got it a lot easier than you  - but tough luck!
Just do it! ☺

We are joined to the Lord.
     We are one spirit with Him.
          We are one spirit with everyone who is joined to Him.

There might be some Christians who don't like me but that's not my problem. If they're joined to Christ they're joined to me and there is nothing they can do about it. They can't kick me out because they didn't kick me in.

You might not agree with me,
but you have to love me!

It's a command!

I might not agree with you
but I have to love you.
I don't have a choice.

It's a command.

Now, don't you feel loved? ☺

Feel the love! (Thanks Col.)

Did you ever stop to think that some of the believers you disagree with most might be living next-door to you in heaven?

Learn to love them *now* by giving thanks for them *now*!

You don't want Jesus to have to stop by your heavenly mansion every day to dry your tears because you wound up living next to me, do you?

LOL!

It's no longer necessary to pray, "Lord make us one".

We are one!

But there's a prayer in **Romans 15** that releases Holy Spirit power to help us live in a greater expression of the unity we already have. This prayer will support us as we "endeavor to keep the unity of the spirit."

*Romans 15:5-6 Now may the God of patience and comfort grant you to be like-minded toward one another, according to Christ Jesus, 6 that you may with one mind and one mouth glorify the God and Father of our Lord Jesus Christ.*

Pray that believers will be likeminded toward one another according to Christ Jesus. Pray that we begin to think about each other the same way that God thinks about us all. Pray that all Christians would begin to concentrate on the things that unify instead of the things that divide. Pray that we would begin to have the same goals and work together towards the same purpose.

Why are we here anyway?

We are not here to build our earthly kingdoms, denominations and organizations, one more glorious than the other. We are here to fulfill the commission that Jesus gave His church before He ascended into Heaven!

*Mark 16:15 And He said to them, "Go into all the world and preach the gospel to every creature."*

No individual ministry, confession or denomination can do this alone. We need all of God's family putting up with each other and working together in love to do this.

Being "likeminded according to Jesus Christ" is not referring to perfect doctrinal unity but being "likeminded according" to the new command that Jesus gave His disciples.

*John 13:34 A new commandment I give to you, that you love one another; as I have loved you, that you also love one another.*

Unity is one of the reasons why revelation knowledge is the biggest need in the body of Christ. If we really KNOW that we are one, there's a greater likelihood that we won't try to kill each other! And that's good!

Currently, I live in Austria where the population is almost 60% Roman Catholic. While I don't agree with every point of Roman Catholic theology, I have many Catholics friends who love Jesus and are genuinely born again and Spirit filled.

They are my brothers and sisters in Christ. I need them.

Some of them realize that they need me too. ☺

I know that some of them think they are the one and only true church of Jesus and that the rest of us are second-class citizens of heaven, but with all due respect, you're probably wrong about some things too!

Disregarding what denomination a child of God belongs to, they belong to the greater body of Christ and we need their gifts, talents and supplies of the Spirit to get the job done that Jesus gave us to fulfill.

Pray for the whole body of Christ –

Catholic,
    Orthodox,
        Protestant,
            Calvinist,
                Arminianist,
                    Evangelical,
                        Pentecostal,
                            Charismatic
(and all of the creative and interesting names used by the many independent churches.)

We are one and we need each other.

Revelation knowledge is the greatest need within the body of Christ and that is why the Holy Spirit inspired Paul to pray several prayers concerning this need.

*Ephesians 1:15-19 Therefore I also, after I heard of your faith in the Lord Jesus and your love for all the saints, 16 do not cease to give thanks for you, making mention of you in my prayers: 17 that the God of our Lord Jesus Christ, the Father of glory, may give to you **the spirit of wisdom and revelation in the knowledge** of Him, 18 **the eyes of your understanding being enlightened; that you may know** what is the hope of His calling, what are the riches of the glory of His inheritance in the saints, 19 and what is the exceeding greatness of His power toward us who believe, according to the working of His mighty power 20 which He worked in Christ when He raised Him from the dead and seated Him at His right hand in the heavenly places,*

**Now get this:** Paul is writing by inspiration of the Holy Spirit. He knows that the folks in Ephesus will get this letter. He knows that they will read the words written on the parchment. He knows that these words are the very words of God but He also knows that they will need the Spirit of wisdom and revelation to understand it.

He prays that "the eyes of our understanding would be enlightened; that we might know…" In other words, there are things we will not KNOW unless the eyes of our heart are enlightened.

That means that we can have a Bible and read it but never really "get it" without the spirit of wisdom and revelation. Not even if it's a 1611 King James Version! "King James Only" people need the Holy Spirit too!

The "spirit of wisdom and revelation" refers to the Holy Spirit revealing truth to our spirit. It can also refer to a heart or spirit that desires and pursues wisdom and revelation. It is a spiritual sensibility by which the eyes of our hearts receive input from the Holy Spirit. It is being enabled to see and hear beyond the realm of mere reason or rational logic.

**The Holy Spirit in our spirit will help us get to know God, His word and His will more intimately.** He will turn the light on – He will enlighten us – He will sharpen our spiritual sensibilities.

As believers, we can know things that others do not know.
      We can see things that others cannot see.
          We can hear things that others cannot hear.

This is the Spirit of wisdom and revelation. This leads to victorious Christian living. Wisdom will be revealed showing us what to do with the knowledge we have gained. Practical insights and applications will flood our hearts. We will KNOW the truth and the truth will make us free.

In this prayer, Paul prays that God would reveal three main things.

**First** he prays that we would know "the hope of His calling". Our purpose and calling in life is found in Jesus' calling. We don't have our own calling – our calling is found in His calling. We don't have "our own ministry" – we are the continuation of His ministry! Every believer has an important part to play in fulfilling God's great love plan for this world.

Knowing God's plan and purpose for our lives is absolutely

essential for our emotional and mental health.

That's why Paul prayed that we would know the HOPE of His calling. There is HOPE in this knowledge. The Greek word translated as "hope" in the New Testament is "elpis". (Not Elvis.) Elpis is a positive, joyful expectation of good things that God has prepared for us!

Finding our calling within His calling fills us with joy and expectation of good things!

**Knowing *why* we are here makes *being* here worthwhile.**

Many Christians have yet to discover the reason why they're living and breathing the air that God created for them to breathe. Having no sense of purpose in life they fall into depression and hopelessness just like ordinary people in the world.

They will never really be happy until they know God's plan for their life and begin walking in the works that He preordained for them.

Pray that the eyes of their heart would be enlightened to know the hope of His calling!

**Secondly**, Paul prays that we would know – by revelation knowledge or heart knowledge – the riches of the glory of God's inheritance in us.

There are two main thoughts here:

We are His inheritance!
He is our inheritance!

He got something.
We got something.

In the Old Testament, God referred to Israel as *His* inheritance.

*Psalm 33:12 Blessed is the nation whose God is the Lord, The people He has chosen as His own inheritance.*

They were *His* inheritance and because of that He gave *them* an inheritance in the Land of Promise.

*Joshua 1:6 Be strong and of good courage, for to this people you shall divide as an inheritance the land which I swore to their fathers to give them.*

Israel was God's inheritance.
God gave Israel an inheritance.

We are God's inheritance
God gave us an inheritance

The two BIG truths that we learn here are:

We are precious and valuable to God!
He has given us precious and valuable riches in Christ.

He got something wonderful!
We got something wonderful!

God purchased you by the blood of Jesus and considers you to be a "good buy". God sees things in you that you have never seen in yourself. You are precious and valuable to God. He got something wonderful when He got you. You need to know that.

A healthy self-image is so important for us as believers. If we see ourselves as worthless or inferior we will never rise to the challenge of fulfilling the destiny that God has for us.

Adlai E. Stevenson said, "It's hard to lead a cavalry charge if you think you look funny on a horse."

We could adapt his witty statement and say, "It's hard to rule and reign in life if you think you look like a loser in the realm of the spirit."

We need to learn how to say with King David:

**Psalm 139:14** *I will praise You, for I am fearfully and wonderfully made; Marvelous are Your works, And that my soul knows very well.*

Our soul needs to KNOW that very well! We need to say it unashamedly as praise unto our God! We are praising His works and we just happen to be one them!

If we speak poorly of ourselves we are speaking poorly of our Creator. He never created anything subpar! You are His masterpiece – unique – one of a kind – authentic God-made goods!

> We are His workmanship!
> We are His handiwork!
> We are His masterpiece created in Christ Jesus!

God only creates good things. In Genesis chapter one, we read time and again, "God said – and it was – and God saw that it was good!"

It never says, "God said – and it was – and God said, " Uh-oh! That doesn't look right!"

After creating man, He took another look at everything He had made and said, "It's *very* good!" The creation of man took everything up a notch on the good scale!

He created you and then recreated you in Christ! You are beautiful, amazing and glorious in Christ!

Pray for the body of Christ that they will KNOW what God inherited in them. Pray that they would see how precious they are to Him!

**We are His inheritance and He has given us an inheritance!**

He has given a rich and complete inheritance in Christ. It's an inheritance that covers every need we will ever have! We are blessed with all spiritual blessings in Christ.

*Ephesians 1:3 Blessed be the God and Father of our Lord Jesus Christ, who has blessed us with every spiritual blessing in the heavenly places in Christ,*

Christ is in us and He is the riches of the glory of our inheritance. He is our hope of glory!

*Colossians 1:27 To them God willed to make known what are the riches of the glory of this mystery among the Gentiles: which is Christ in you, the hope of glory.*

We are heirs of God and joint-heirs with Jesus!

*Romans 8:16-17a The Spirit Himself bears witness with our spirit that we are children of God, 17 and if children, then heirs — heirs of God and joint heirs with Christ*

What a rich and glorious inheritance!

Ours is a life of blessing –
   a life of abundance –
      a life of victory!
         We need to KNOW that!

**Lastly**, Paul prays that we would KNOW the exceeding greatness of His power that is working in us, for us and through us.

It is as if Paul struggled to find words big enough to describe the power that is available to every believer. The same power that raised Jesus from the dead is now working in you and me.

We need to KNOW that there is resurrection power in us when we are facing the trials of life. We need to see by revelation that we never lack for power or ability to perform the things that God has called us to do.

There is power for your marriage.
There is power for your business.
There is power for your school days.
There is power for your ministry in Christ.
There is power to save, heal and deliver and that power is working in you right now!

Pray for your brothers and sisters that they would know – have a revelation of – the resurrection power of Jesus that's working in them!

Many believers live and die never knowing God's plan and purpose for their lives. Others go around with their head hanging down feeling unworthy to stand up and speak the words of life to this needy world. And still others have no idea of the resurrection power that is available to them. As long as this is the case, the body of Christ will be weak, ineffective and barely keep pace with the blind religions of the nations that God has called us to reach.

One of the biggest and most important occupations for us as Christians is to discover what God has done for us in Christ, take possession of it by faith, and learn how to practically apply it in our lives.

We can pray this prayer for ourselves and for the body of Christ. You can put *your* name in this prayer. In other words you can pray:

"Father, I ask You to give me the spirit of wisdom and revelation in the knowledge of Yourself, that the eyes of my understanding may be enlightened to know You more, that I might know what the hope of Your calling is and what the riches of the glory of Your inheritance in me is and what the exceeding greatness of Your power toward me who believes is."

Pray this prayer for your church and for the entire body of Christ as well. You can ask God to give your pastor and your co-workers in the church the spirit of wisdom and revelation in the knowledge of God.

This is a Holy Spirit inspired prayer and you can be sure that God will always answer it with a "yes".

When we begin to KNOW how much power is working in us, for us and potentially through us, it will be a great day for the kingdom of God and for world evangelism! Pray that this be REVEALED to the heart of every believer!

# 8. MORE REVELATION

Another prayer for revelation knowledge is found two chapters later in Ephesians.

***Ephesians 3:14-19*** *For this reason I bow my knees to the Father of our Lord Jesus Christ, 15 from whom the whole family in heaven and earth is named, 16 that He would grant you, according to the riches of His glory, to be strengthened with might through His Spirit in the inner man, 17 that Christ may dwell in your hearts through faith; that you, being rooted and grounded in love, 18 may be able to comprehend with all the saints what is the width and length and depth and height — 19 to know the love of Christ which passes knowledge; that you may be filled with all the fullness of God.*

We can also pray this prayer for ourselves and for the body of Christ. Lord, strengthen us with might by your Spirit in our inner man! God will always say yes to this prayer!

When I pray this for our church and for other believers I try to imagine that power rising up within them right at that moment. If they are driving to work or school – already in work or school – or on vacation in the Islands – anywhere they might be – I try to imagine that power filling and strengthening them. I see them strengthened and being bold and confident in all that they have to do – even if it's just getting some rest and a tan on the beach!

We can release God's strength and impart the power of the Holy

Spirit to the body of Christ through this prayer!

Paul also prays that the church would be rooted and grounded in love. We will grow strong and be healthy inwardly and outwardly if we are planted deeply in the soil of God's love.

He prays we would UNDERSTAND with all saints
    how wide,
        how long,
            how deep
                and how high God's love is.

He asks the Father to help us KNOW the love of Christ, which passes knowledge.

Get it? He prays that we would know something that is beyond our ability to know. No matter how much we think we know about God's love, there is much more to learn. His love goes far beyond our mental abilities to fathom. This prayer shows us that we can know things with our heart that our minds can only marvel at.

We will never really be stabile, secure and strong in our faith until we realize that God loves us unequivocally. His love for us is perfect, unchanging, unconditional, never ending and fail proof.

Too many Christians live the roller-coaster kind of Christianity that never achieves full maturity. One day they're up and the next day they're down. A revelation of God's love will keep us growing and going from glory to glory.

We need to know this love intimately and personally. I'm not talking about the general knowledge that "God loves everybody". It needs to be real to us. We need to see it, hear it and know it in our hearts. We need to be rooted and grounded in this love. We need to understand that no matter what happens God will never, ever, ever stop loving us with all of His perfect love!

Paul says that when we KNOW the love of Christ, we will be filled with the very fullness of God.

Think of it!
You – FILLED with all the fullness of God!
Me – FILLED with all the fullness of God!

God is love. To be filled with the fullness of God is to be filled with the fullness of His love!

If we know God's love and are conscious that His love resides in us at all times then we will also be filled with everything that God can fill us with. This truth is beyond our ability to comprehend.

That's why revelation is the greatest need in the body of Christ.

The Christian life is a supernatural life. Many people are trying to live it by their own power and their own mental abilities and are failing miserably. Because of that, unbelievers think of Christianity as if it were nothing more than one of the many world religions. But Christianity is not first and foremost a religion. It is the only answer for this world. It is the revelation of God's eternal, infinite love for this broken, hurting world. We need to know God's love until it begins to fill and permeate every aspect of our lives.

The more we KNOW God's love, the more we will walk in freedom from fear and worry.

*1 John 4:18 There is no fear in love; but perfect love casts out fear, because fear involves torment. But he who fears has not been made perfect in love.*

Insecurity melts away. Worries disappear. Fear flees! His love for us never fails and never comes to an end.

*1 Corinthians 13:8a  Love never fails [it never fades nor ends].*
*AMP*

As the revelation of His love increasingly dawns upon our hearts we will be supernaturally compelled to reach out to others with this love. We'll see their lost state and their need for Christ through His eyes of love and compassion. Instead of walking through life oblivious to the needs of others, His love in us will compel us to see and do something about it.

*2 Corinthians 5:14 a For the love of Christ compels us…*

Let's pray for our brothers and sisters in Christ
that they will come to KNOW God's love
in an ever higher, deeper, longer and wider
REVELATION.

Loving God, knowing that He loves you and loving others is the essence of what this thing is all about! Cooper Beatty, one of my professors in Bible College said, "90% of good theology is about loving God and loving people."

God wants us to experience His love, grow in His love and share His love with everyone we meet!

**Philippians 1:9** *And this is my prayer: that your love may abound more and more in knowledge and depth of insight,* **(NIV)**

Again, He wants us to grow in the KNOWLEDGE of His love! The Luther translation of this verse reads, *"And I pray that your love would be ever richer in knowledge and every experience."* God wants us to KNOW and experience His love in an ever increasing manner – everywhere we go and in everything we do! Revelation transforms information into experiential knowledge!

Pray this for your family in Christ. Pray this for the body. Pray this wonderful Holy Spirit inspired prayer daily for your brothers and sisters in Christ.

Saturate yourself in God's love. Continue in His love. Let God put His loving arms around you and hold you closely. You mean so very much to Him! You are precious. You are the apple of His eye. You are His treasured possession. You are His love child and He rejoices over you!

Here's another prayer for revelation knowledge:

**Colossians 1:9-12** *For this reason we also, since the day we heard it, do not cease to pray for you, and to ask that you may be filled with the knowledge of His will in all wisdom and spiritual understanding; 10 that you may walk worthy of the Lord, fully pleasing Him, being fruitful in every good work and increasing in the knowledge of God; 11 strengthened with all might, according to His glorious power, for all patience and longsuffering with joy; 12 giving thanks to the Father who has qualified us to be partakers of the inheritance of the saints in the light.*

Did you notice how many blessings are connected to revelation knowledge? If we are filled with the KNOWLEDGE of His will in all WISDOM and spiritual UNDERSTANDING we will:

Live a life that is pleasing to the Father,
  be fruitful in every good work,
    grow in the knowledge of God,
      be strengthened with His glorious power,
        grow in patience,
          be filled with joy,
            be thankful,
              and partake of our inheritance!

Paul's prayers for the church are recorded in detail. But we have no information at all about how he prayed for the world. He said that he prayed for the unbelieving Jews to be saved but we are given no further information about that prayer.

That should tell us something concerning what God wants us to be praying about.

In this Holy Spirit inspired prayer in Colossians, Paul prays that we would be filled with the KNOWLEDGE of God's will.

The Greek word translated as "knowledge" in this verse is *"epignosis"*. It means "precise and correct knowledge". (Thayers) It means "to know thoroughly, to recognize a thing to be what it really is". (Vine's)

Knowing things in the sense of revelation knowledge will transform our lives. Instead of being conformed to this world we will begin to transform our world. When we recognize God's word to be what it really is, the door to freedom will open and we will walk through it!

Many wonder, "What is God's will for my life?" but never really find out what it is. We can help them! We can strive for them in prayer that they might attain to a full knowledge of God's will and have the grace they need to walk in it.

Joy, peace, wisdom, health, prosperity, meaningful relationships and power to be witnesses for Christ are aspects of God's perfect will for all of His children! God has a good plan and purpose for the life of every Christian!

Many have heard these things but are still wavering in their hearts. We can pray that they will be filled with revelation knowledge – the precise and correct knowledge – a thorough knowledge – of His perfect will for their lives.

Paul prays that we would "walk worthy of the Lord to all pleasing." There are Christians struggling right now to overcome things in their lives that do not please God. They have used up their strength and have failed. Join your faith to theirs in prayer and support them. Help them walk in the victory that Jesus purchased for them. Victory over sinful habits begins with revelation!

Paul also prays that the Colossians would be "fruitful in every good work!" Do you know someone who is doing something good for God? Anyone who is working for the Lord knows that there can be both spiritual and natural resistance. Some are working so hard but seeing very little fruit. It can be so frustrating to work and work and see no results! There might be a thousand reasons why things aren't working, but we can partner with them in prayer that they would be fruitful in every good work. God will help them, change things, reveal things, break barriers, open doors, grant supernatural favor and cause things to grow if we will pray!

Another part of this prayer request for the body of Christ is that they would grow in the knowledge of God. There are many disciplines that lead to growing in the knowledge of God such as Bible reading, attending church, praying, fasting, witnessing and so on. But apparently our prayers for the family of God can also help them grow in the knowledge of God.

We are in this together. My prayers help you and your prayers help me. It's not just about what we ourselves do but also what we do together – what we do for one another – that helps us grow!

Paul prays further that we would be "strengthened with all might, according to His glorious power, for all patience and longsuffering with joy;" You can release power into believer's lives by praying like this. Suddenly they will have the extra strength to walk in patience, longsuffering and joy.

We all need that!
Or am I the only one? ☺

The main purpose of this prayer is to support the spiritual growth and maturity of the church. Often churches rely solely on teaching and training programs to bring about spiritual growth and maturity.

Teaching and training is important but we need to preface these things, fill them and follow them up with prayer. This prayer in Colossians is a biblical example of how to pray for spiritual growth and maturity in the lives of believers.

Use it.
    Pray it.
        Believe it.
            Reach out with it!

I am convinced that the principle of sowing and reaping works here as well. If you pray for others, you will receive a harvest of people who are praying for you. If the whole body of Christ would begin to act upon the "Priority Number One in Prayer" there would be exponential growth and harvest taking place in our personal lives and in our ministries!

Lastly, in his prayer for the Church in Colossae, Paul prays that they would give thanks to the Father who has made them fit to be partakers of the inheritance of the saints in light. In other words, he prays that believers would begin to actively express their thankfulness to God for everything He has done for them in Christ. A thankful heart is a faith-filled and joyful heart. Giving thanks is a key to receiving the blessings of our inheritance in Christ.

This prayer has the power to change a believer's attitude from that of grumbling and complaining to one of rejoicing and thanksgiving. Joy and thankfulness are attractive to this broken world filled with sorrow, bad news, negative attitudes and depression.

Do you know a Christian "complainer" or a church member who is a chronic critic? This is a good prayer for them!

Don't complain about the complainers.
Don't just criticize the critics.
Pray for them!

# 9. PAUL'S PRAYER REQUESTS

In this chapter we will read some of Paul's personal prayer requests. They are prayers that we can still make use of today – not praying for Paul – he doesn't need our prayers anymore – but in praying for our leaders in the body of Christ.

*Ephesians 6:18 praying always with all prayer and supplication in the Spirit, being watchful to this end with all perseverance and supplication for all the saints 19 and for me, that utterance may be given to me, that I may open my mouth boldly to make known the mystery of the gospel, 20 for which I am an ambassador in chains; that in it I may speak boldly, as I ought to speak.*

I'm always encouraged by the fact that Paul requested prayer on numerous occasions. He wasn't ashamed to admit that he needed the prayer support of the body of Christ.

I need it.
    You need it.
        We all need it.
            Just admit it.

He asked that they would pray for him that:

- Utterance would be given him
- That he would preach boldly
- That the mystery of the gospel would be revealed through his ministry.

Many people criticize pastors and ministers when what they should be doing is praying for them. If we don't like our pastor's preaching, it might be more our fault than theirs! Have we been praying for them or criticising and gossiping about them?

Good question.

Our prayers for the leadership in the body of Christ can have an impact on how well their ministry is received by others AND BY US! If we've prayed in faith and believe that God has answered our prayer, then we will go to church with a different attitude! We will go expecting to receive and I guarantee you, God will not disappoint us!

Let's pray that God would give our leaders boldness and that revelation would flow to them and through them!

Pray that God would give them utterance.

Utterance?

"What's utterance?", you ask.

It has to do with uttering.

The Greek word translated as "utterance" is *"logos"* which basically means "word". Among other things, it means communication, concepts, skill, style and practice in speaking.

There is a divine element and a human element to preaching and teaching. The anointing is always perfect but the human vessel through which it flows is not. The good news is that the human element can be improved. And our prayers can help it improve!

Let's pray that God would give pastors utterance. It's a fun word to use, isn't it?

> Give them utterance, Oh Lord!
> Help them utter, dear Father!
> Grant them greater utterance in all their uttering.
> May their utterance be glorious as they utter your glories!
> Amen!

Their preaching and teaching skills will improve as we pray for them and believe God. That's a prayer that will help, bless and edify the whole church!

But like I said, it could be that this prayer will help us just as much as our pastors. It might be a case like that of Mark Twain who purportedly said, "When I was a boy of fourteen, my father was so ignorant I could hardly stand to have the old man around. But when I got to be twenty-one, I was astonished at how much he had learned in seven years." Maybe it was the younger Mr. Twain that had learned so much – and maybe it will be us who are changed by this prayer.

"Give them utterance, Lord!" ☺

**Romans 15:30** *Now I beg you, brethren, through the Lord Jesus Christ, and through the love of the Spirit, that you strive together with me in prayers to God for me, 31 that I may be delivered from those in Judea who do not believe, and that my service for Jerusalem may be acceptable to the saints, 32 that I may come to you with joy by the will of God, and may be refreshed together with you.*

This is a great prayer for leaders. Paul covers a lot of the needs that every leader faces in this prayer request.

One of the those requests was for supernatural protection. Ministers are on the front lines. There is an enemy who wants to destroy them and their families. You can surround them with a hedge of protection by your prayers!

He also asked them to pray that his ministry would be accepted by the saints. The effectiveness of a ministry is not based solely on what the minister does. People must have open and receptive hearts to profit from the gift of God in their lives.

Jesus couldn't do any mighty works in His hometown because the people were offended and didn't believe Him. Notice these verses in Mark:

**Mark 6:3b** *They were offended at Him.*

**Mark 6:6a** *He marveled because of their unbelief.*

**Mark 6:5a** *He could do no mighty work there.*

Because they were offended, they didn't believe. Because they didn't believe, He COULDN'T do any mighty works there. They didn't think of Him as being anyone special and therefore they didn't open their hearts to receive from Him. How much more could that be the case with regular folks like us?

Pray that people will open their hearts to receive from the leaders that Jesus placed in His Church.

And be open yourself.

Not just for the exciting sermons but also for the corrective ones.

Thank you for your enthusiastic amen! ☺

Paul also asked them to pray that he might be refreshed! Ministers need refreshing. When they are refreshed, their ministry will be fresh! It'll be a blessing and an encouragement to you and your church! Be a source of refreshing and pray for them! Ask God to give them a fresh anointing and to fill them afresh with the Holy Spirit.

**Colossians 4:3** *meanwhile praying also for us, that God would open to us a door for the word, to speak the mystery of Christ, for which I am also in chains, 4 that I may make it manifest, as I ought to speak.*

Paul requests prayer again!

He asked the believers in Colossae to pray that God would open a door for him to speak the mystery of Christ. This is a great prayer to pray for those in missionary, evangelistic, prophetic or other kinds of travelling ministries.

**"God, I ask you to open doors for them to preach and teach your word, in Jesus' Name! Amen."**

God is able to open doors that no man can close. There are areas of the world right now that are closed to the gospel. Pray that God would open doors, grant favor, change laws and make a way for believers and ministers in those countries to preach the good news!

Paul also asked them to pray that he would "make the gospel

manifest as he ought to speak". To make something manifest means to make it so clear that all those who are hearing it can see and understand what is being said.

He wanted to connect with those to whom he was preaching.

Pray that ministers would connect with their audience. Pray that they would be able to reach the hearts of those they are ministering to. Pray that the word of God would hit the target at which it is being aimed!

Paul wanted his hearers to get the revelation of what he was preaching. Only the Holy Spirit can reveal truth to the heart of a person. A preacher may preach to people but the Holy Spirit must reveal truth to them. Pray for increased anointing upon the preachers and teachers in the body of Christ!

Paul needed this kind of prayer.
   I need this kind of prayer.
      Your pastor needs this kind of prayer.

Sometimes people think that it's easy to stand up and preach and teach the word!

### It's not!

It is a great challenge and anyone who's ever done it knows what I'm talking about.

Yes, it's wonderful and it's a great honor. But it's also a huge responsibility. Paul asked them to pray that he might make the mystery of Christ manifest AS HE OUGHT. Why? Because it's an awe-inspiring responsibility! It's not always easy and its not always fun! Without God's help we cannot do it as we ought!

Your pastor probably needs your prayers more than he needs your advice. Just sayin'.

**1Thessalonians 5:25** Brethren, *pray for us*.

Stop grumbling and just pray for them!

      ☺              ☺              ☺

(Did you pray for them yet?)

***2 Thessalonians 3:1** Finally, brethren, pray for us, that the word of the Lord may run swiftly and be glorified, just as it is with you,*

Pray that the Holy Spirit would create an atmosphere filled with liberty and freedom.  Pray that the word would flow freely from the heart of the preacher into the heart of the listener.

Pray that it would bring glory to God.

Pray that it will produce fruit,
      honor God,
            change lives,
                  bring salvation,
                        make disciples
                              and equip people
                                    for the work
                                          of the ministry!

***Hebrews 13:18-19** Pray for us; for we are confident that we have a good conscience, in all things desiring to live honorably. 19 But I especially urge you to do this, that I may be restored to you the sooner.*

The minister who wrote to the Hebrews desired to live honestly and honorably. I believe that all ministers desire to live honestly and honorably, don't you? I know there have been some bad apples in the basket but I believe that most ministers want to do right and live right.

But that desire has to be translated into doing.

I refuse to believe that any minister who has ever fallen wanted to fall. I don't believe they wanted to disgrace God, hurt their families, disappoint people or wreck churches.

I just refuse to believe that.

But those who stand in ministry offices are on the front lines of this spiritual battle. If the enemy can bring them down, he will bring others down with them. Knowing this should create a desire in us to strengthen the hands of those who are in the ministry.

Instead of criticizing them and being a part of the problem, we should pray for them and be a part of the answer! Pray that God would give them the grace that they need to stand strong against the attacks and temptations of the enemy. Your prayer might be the one thing standing between them and shipwreck! Don't let them fall. Do what you can!

Pray for them!
　　Strengthen them!
　　　　Encourage them!
　　　　　　Lift up their hands!
　　　　　　　　Your prayers make tremendous power available.

Paul had great confidence in the prayers of the body of Christ. He coveted their prayers and let them know how thankful he was that they prayed for him. The prayers of the saints were a source of strength for him and helped him accomplish God's purpose for his life.

**2 Corinthians 1:11** *you also helping together in prayer for us, that thanks may be given by many persons on our behalf for the gift granted to us through many.*

Prayer really helps!
Never forget that!

When you pray for a minister or a ministry you are taking an active role in their ministry. You are helping Jesus as He works through them. You're supporting them as they fight the good fight of faith. The whole church – the body of Christ will benefit from that! Your help may go unnoticed by everyone else but God sees it and the ministry you are praying for will experience real help and support.

Never think that your prayers are insignificant. They are very significant!

**Philippians 1:19** *For I know that this will turn out for my deliverance through your prayer and the supply of the Spirit of Jesus Christ,*

Listen to that confidence! I KNOW that your prayers are going to make the difference for me right here and right now!

**Philemon 1:22** *But, meanwhile, also prepare a guest room for me, for I trust that through your prayers I shall be granted to you.*

Paul was in prison but he was so confident in Philemon's prayers that he said, "Get a room ready for me because I know I'll be getting out soon." He said, "I trust that your prayers are going to get the job done!" (paraphrased)

> The prayers of God's people are powerful.
> Never underestimate the power of your prayers.
> Believe that God hears you when you pray.
> Believe that He is responding to your requests.
> You have power with God in the Name of Jesus!

We can make the difference in the body of Christ and in the lives of our leaders. This is world changing. This will impact eternity! This will further the cause. This will open doors, break down barriers and help fill our nations with the KNOWLEDGE of God's glory!

# 10. SEVEN REASONS PLUS

I said I would do it and here it is; more reasons why prayer for the body of Christ is priority number one in prayer. I actually list eight reasons but seven sounds more spiritual than eight so here are "Seven Reasons Plus". Bear with me. Thanks. ☺

This is not an all-inclusive list and the reasons are not listed in order of importance.

**Reason One: Because God said so!**

*Galatians 6:10 Therefore, as we have opportunity, let us do good to all, especially to those who are of the household of faith.*

Prayer is "doing good" and God said that we should make it our priority to do good to those of the household of faith.

God said it! We should do it.

That's enough reason right there! But wait – there's more!

**Reason Two: Because of our commission!**

*Mark 16:15-16 And He said to them, "Go into all the world and preach the gospel to every creature. 16 He who believes and is baptized will be saved; but he who does not believe will be condemned.*

What Jesus said to them back then, He is saying to us today! "Go into all the world!" We have the most important job in the universe.

The salvation of humanity is in our hands. The lost are not saved by our prayers but by hearing and believing the Gospel!

It's good and right to pray for the government, for Israel and for the lost but if they never hear the Gospel all those prayers will have been little more than wasted breath. They will have been vain wishes, void of results.

*1 Corinthians 1:21 For since, in the wisdom of God, the world through wisdom did not know God, it pleased God through the foolishness of the message preached to save those who believe.*

Sitting in the church and praying for the lost is easy but it will never save them. We have to get out there and share the life saving, glorious, powerful Gospel of Jesus!

So much of the body of Christ is too consumed and distracted with their own problems to tell anyone else about Jesus. The church has to be blessed and empowered to shine as the light she is in this dark world.

Prayer releases blessing and power!

The job that Jesus has left us is so big and so awesome that we need all of God's help to get it done. Prayer is one way that we get that help.

Never forget this: When the body of Christ is blessed, the world will automatically be blessed.

You can be sure of it.

### Reason Three: Because it's good for us!

*Matthew 6:33 But seek first the kingdom of God and His righteousness, and all these things shall be added to you.*

Seek FIRST – and then – ALL these things will be added to YOU.

Jesus is our King and those who believe in Him are citizens of His Kingdom. Making it a priority to pray for the body of Christ is one way to "seek first" the Kingdom of God. Let's make His priorities our priorities.

When God's Kingdom is our number one priority He has promised to give us all the things that we need.

Yes, I know that you have needs. So do I. And praying for the body is one way to get our needs met. Praying for the saints is good for the saints and good for us!

We will reap what we have sown! If we sow prayer we will reap prayer.

I'm absolutely sure that God is speaking to someone right now on your behalf. He's raising up people to pray for you right now because you have been faithful to pray for His people.

**Reason Four: Because we need one another!**

*1 Corinthians 12:21-22 And the eye cannot say to the hand, "I have no need of you"; nor again the head to the feet, "I have no need of you." 22 No, much rather, those members of the body which seem to be weaker are necessary.*

God has placed us in the body of Christ as He saw fit!

He didn't even ask our opinion about it.

We don't get to choose what church we want to attend! God chose it for us. We need to hook up with His plans if we want to succeed in life. Let's not be church hoppers. Many gifted people go from one church to the next and never really grow up in Christ. Sadly, they will never fulfill their divine destiny because they are not where God wants them and they never put down any roots.

God placed us in the body. He set us in the church that is best suited to help us grow up and fulfill His plans and purposes for our lives.

And we need one another to do that! We are connected to one another in the spirit.

I need you and you need me.

*1 Corinthians 6:17 But he who is joined to the Lord is one spirit with Him.*

In a very real sense, my success is based partly on your success and your success is based partly on my success. If you're weak and messed up that makes me at least a little weak and messed up too. If I'm weak and messed up – well, that doesn't help you either!

*1 Corinthians 12:26 And if one member suffers, all the members suffer with it; or if one member is honored, all the members rejoice with it.*

It's in my own best interest to pray for you. It is in your best interest to pray for me and for the rest of the body of Christ. We can strengthen and support one another through prayer. Together we are strong. Together we will get the job done.

### Reason Five: Because Jesus told us to love one another!

*John 13:34-35 A new commandment I give to you, that you love one another; as I have loved you, that you also love one another. 35 By this all will know that you are My disciples, if you have love for one another."*

**Jesus told us to love one another,
not fight and criticize one another.**

How will the world know that we are truly His disciples?

By our love for one another!

The way that some Christians speak in public about their brothers and sisters is so shameful and dishonoring. YouTube, Facebook and other public "social" platforms are filled with Christians hating and berating one another. Of course there is a place for criticism and correction but it shouldn't be hateful, mean-hearted and nasty!

And it shouldn't be in public before an unbelieving world!

If you've done this, then repent and God will forgive you! ☺

I read about a survey that was conducted where people were asked, "What do you think of Jesus?" The people used words like, "merciful, wise, great teacher, kind, friendly, generous" and so on to describe Him. The surveyors then asked, "What do you think of the church?" Lots of people wrinkled their noses and said things like, "narrow minded, hateful, bigoted, mean-hearted, obsolete, irrelevant" and so on.

102

What was the difference? I don't believe that it's primarily because of our beliefs concerning abortion or sexuality. I believe it's mainly because of how we treat one another. Who would want to be part of a club that kills and mutilates it's own members?

When we pray for one another our love for one another will grow.

I know. It happened to me. I love the body of Christ more than ever! The Bride of Jesus is so beautiful; so radiant and glorious. I love the Catholics. I love the Orthodox. I love the Protestants. I love the Evangelicals. I love the Calvinists. I love the Arminianists. I love the Pentecostals. I love the Charismatics! I love everyone who is born again!

I don't necessarily agree with every point of their doctrine but I love them. My spiritual father taught me, "You can disagree without being disagreeable!" We can disagree with one another but we still have to love one another!

Love is not just a word, it's an action. Love is something we do.

Praying is doing something.
Praying is loving someone.

All men will know that we are Jesus' disciples because of our love for one another.

## Reason Six: Because prayer unifies and unity is powerful!

*Acts 1:14 These all continued with one accord in prayer and supplication*

*Acts 2:1 When the Day of Pentecost had fully come, they were all with one accord in one place.*

*Acts 4:24 So when they heard that, they raised their voice to God with one accord and said…*

Nothing unifies like prayer! We might not agree on everything but we do agree that prayer is powerful.

We do agree that everyone needs Jesus!
We do agree that we all need God's help.
We do agree that God hears and answers prayers.

Walls fall down and the sweet ointment of unity begins to flow when we pray with and for one another.

*Psalm 133:1 Behold, how good and how pleasant it is for brethren to dwell together in unity! 2 It is like the precious oil upon the head, running down on the beard, The beard of Aaron, running down on the edge of his garments. 3 It is like the dew of Hermon, descending upon the mountains of Zion; For there the Lord commanded the blessing – Life forevermore.*

This is where the blessing is poured out! When we get together in unity and love it is awesome. It is precious. There's an anointing that flows over the whole body of Christ! All the way down to the tips of the toes!

Unity is powerful.
    Unity makes everything possible.
        Together we can win the world for Jesus!

*Genesis 11:6 And the Lord said, "Indeed the people are one and they all have one language, and this is what they begin to do; now nothing that they propose to do will be withheld from them.*

The problem in Babel wasn't that they were unified.

The problem was that they were disobedient. God told them to be fruitful, multiply and fill the earth but they decided they weren't going to do that. They willfully chose to stay right there in Babel and do what they wanted. **(see Genesis 9:7 & 11:4)**

Nonetheless, note the power of unity! Nothing they proposed to do would be impossible for them! If that's the case in the negative, how much more is it so in the positive. If unity works for people who are disobedient, how much more will it work for those who are obeying God and seeking to fulfill His purposes!

Unity is powerful and can be a very good thing! When we are unified we are stronger. When we are unified nothing that we propose will be impossible.

I propose we do more to reach the world for Jesus right now and discuss all the theological intricacies and side issues later – when we're all in heaven. We'll have more time for it then and we'll all know more than we do now.

Unity makes it possible for us to glorify the God and Father of our Lord Jesus Christ in this world.

**Romans 15:5-6** *Now may the God of patience and comfort grant you to be like-minded toward one another, according to Christ Jesus, 6 that you may with one mind and one mouth glorify the God and Father of our Lord Jesus Christ.*

Being likeminded according to Christ Jesus is being likeminded according to His love. It is keeping Him as the central focus of our fellowships, discussions, plans and purposes.

Jesus gave us His glory and that glory has made us one.

**John 17:22-23** *And the glory which You gave Me I have given them, that they may be one just as We are one: 23 I in them, and You in Me; that they may be made perfect in one, and that the world may know that You have sent Me, and have loved them as You have loved Me.*

GLORY!

When we pray for one another that glory is released; that glory becomes visible and active in the world. It's the glory of God's love in us and our unity in Christ that will persuade the world that Jesus Christ has come from the Father.

Nothing unifies like prayer and unity is powerful!

**Reason Seven: Because we are family!**

**Ephesians 3:14-16** *For this reason I bow my knees to the Father of our Lord Jesus Christ, 15 from whom the whole family in heaven and earth is named, 16 that He would grant you, according to the riches of His glory, to be strengthened with might through His Spirit in the inner man,*

We are family and many of our brothers and sisters are suffering

Many are suffering with sickness.
Many are suffering persecution.
Many are suffering with marriage problems.
Many are suffering with financial problems.
Many are suffering with mental health issues.

Many are suffering because their children are away from God. Many are suffering with worry, fear and insecurity.

There's so much suffering in our family.

But we can help.

Prayer helps. (Am I repeating myself again?)

Let's lift up our voices for our brothers and sisters in Christ. This isn't just a club or a business or an organization. This is family.

Families stick together.
    Families help each other.
        Families are there for each other.

Someone once said, "The family that prays together, stays together". How true.

If the family is strong, blessed, healthy and full of the Holy Spirit, we will be much more efficient in reaching our world for Christ.

Healthy and blessed marriages, families, relationships, finances, businesses, workers, teachers, students, children etc. are a powerful witness to the world.

**PLUS: Because Jesus is our example!**

**John 17:9** I pray for them. I do not pray for the world but for those whom You have given Me, for they are Yours.

In the Garden of Gethsemane Jesus prayed for His disciples and for those who would believe because of their witness. He prayed for believers.

Jesus is our example.

We are called to walk even as He walked.

*1 John 2:6 He who says he abides in Him ought himself also to walk just as He walked.*

We can walk and pray
    or kneel and pray
        or stand on our heads and pray. ☺

But if we want to follow Jesus' example in prayer, we'll make prayer for believers our top priority.

Several prayers of Jesus are recorded in the Gospels but not one of them was a prayer for the lost. When He saw the lost and scattered multitudes He didn't pray for them. He prayed that the Lord of the harvest would send laborers to them!

When Jesus knew that Peter was going to be attacked by the enemy, He prayed for Him. And He knew that that prayer would make the difference in Peter's life.

*Luke 22:31-32 And the Lord said, "Simon, Simon! Indeed, Satan has asked for you, that he may sift you as wheat. 32 But I have prayed for you, that your faith should not fail; and when you have returned to Me, strengthen your brethren."*

Peter went on to be the great Apostle who opened the door for the Gospel to both the Jews and the Gentiles! But it could have been different. He could have given in to discouragement or depression and quit. Jesus' prayer supported him and helped him overcome the attack!

How many spiritual attacks could have been avoided, thwarted or rendered powerless if only someone had prayed!

Let's follow Jesus' example and pray for His followers!

Hopefully these seven plus reasons have convinced you that praying for your brothers and sisters in Christ is priority number one in prayer.

Hopefully they have encouraged and challenged you to begin praying more for your pastor, those in your church and for the entire body of Christ.

# 11. HOW TO PRAY

***Ephesians 6:18*** *praying always with all prayer and supplication in the Spirit, being watchful to this end with all perseverance and supplication for all the saints*

The New Testament teaches us that there are various kinds of prayer.

The NIV translates Ephesians 6:18 like this:

***Ephesians 6:18a*** *And pray in the Spirit on all occasions with all kinds of prayers and requests.*

There are different kinds of prayers for different kinds of situations. Each one of the different kinds of prayer has a specific purpose and is governed by specific rules. We need to learn about the different kinds of prayers and their purposes and rules. There are many good books available on the various kinds of prayer and how to pray. That goes beyond the scope of this book but here are a few comments and some helpful instructions.

## The Prayer of Faith

The prayer of faith is a prayer based upon God's promises in the Bible. We find a promise and bring it to God in faith, trusting Him to do what He said He would do.

***Numbers 23:19*** *God is not a man, that He should lie, Nor a son of man, that He should repent. Has He said, and will He not do? Or has He spoken, and will He not make it good?*

Everything that God has promised He will surely do. We can pray confidently when our prayers are founded on the word of God.

In the prayer of faith, we have to believe that we received the answer to our request the moment we prayed. We receive it or take it by faith. Afterward we give thanks and praise to God, joyfully expecting to see it come to pass. We shall have it! Jesus promised!

*Mark 11:24 Therefore I tell you, whatever you ask for in prayer, believe that you have received it, and it will be yours.*

## The Prayer of Petition

The prayer or petition is simply a prayer in which we ask and keep on asking for something. There are some kinds of prayer where you ask only once and then thank God for the answer. There are other kinds of prayer where we need to continue to ask, seek, knock and petition God.

In **Matthew 7:7** Jesus said, "Ask and it shall be given to you." The Amplified Translation expresses the continual sense of the Greek verb.

*Matthew 7:7a Ask and keep on asking and it will be given to you. AMP*

If we are asking God to do something for us, normally the prayer of faith is sufficient. We ask, we believe we received it and we give thanks! But if we are praying for others or about situations involving other people, we often have to "ask and keep on asking".

It is not that we have to coax God or talk Him into doing something. He is always ready to hear and answer. But the people we are praying for can change from one moment to the next. Because of their free will we have to be persistent until we see the answer.

Never give up on people. God didn't give up on us and we shouldn't give up on others. There's always hope with Him.

## The Prayer of Agreement

The prayer of agreement requires that two people come together and ask God for the same exact thing. Their agreement must be based upon the word of God and their prayer must be unified by mutual faith. Having a prayer partner can be a great help! We can strengthen one another by adding our faith together and targeting a specific need.

If you are married – and your spouse is a believer – you have a built-in prayer partner to agree with you in prayer.

I remember when an older widower in the church remarried. Some folks asked him why, at the age of 72, he was getting married again. He said, "Because the Bible says that one will chase a thousand and two will chase ten thousand."

## Good answer!

When we agree in prayer, our prayers are exponentially more powerful!

**Matthew 18:19** *Again, I tell you that if two of you on earth agree about anything you ask for, it will be done for you by my Father in heaven.*

In this promise we see the power of unity all over again! Thank God for the power of unity and the power of agreement in prayer!

## The Prayer of Supplication

**Philippians 4:6-7** *Do not be anxious about anything, but in everything, by prayer and supplication, with thanksgiving, present your requests to God. 7 And the peace of God, which transcends all understanding, will guard your hearts and your minds in Christ Jesus.*

The prayer of supplication can either be a prayer of petition, the prayer of faith or in reality any other kind of prayer. It is a fervent and heartfelt prayer. We bring our heartfelt needs to the Lord and He grants us peace!

Earlier we saw that Paul prayed for his countrymen who were not yet saved.

**Romans 10:1** *Brethren, my heart's desire and prayer to God for Israel is that they may be saved.*

The Greek word for "prayer" in **Romans 10:1** is *"deesis"*. In other verses where this word is found it is translated as supplication. Paul makes it plain that this need, this request was a deeply felt desire of his heart.

In other Bible translations "my heart's desire" is translated as:

*"The longing of my heart"* – The Living Bible
*"I want it with all of my heart"* – The Message Bible
*"My deepest desire"* – Complete Jewish Bible
*"The delight of my own heart"* – Darby Bible
*"The will of my heart"* – Douay-Rheims Bible
*"The thing I want most"* – New Century Version
*"With all my heart I long for"* – New International Reader's Version

That's what a prayer of supplication is. It is a deep desire. It is something that you long for. It's something that you want with all of your heart!

Remember, if it touches your heart, it touches the heart of God!

Norvel Hayes said, "You've got to pray like a house on fire and put your whole heart into it. Pray until God comes and when He comes, you can have whatever He has."

James said that the prayer of supplication is powerful and effective.

**James 5:16** *The prayer (deesis - supplication) of a righteous man is powerful and effective.*

### The Prayer of Intercession

The prayer of intercession involves praying for someone who does not have the right to approach the throne of God. As God's own children, we have the right to come to the Father in the Name of Jesus. Jesus gave us authority to use His Name in prayer. Those who are not yet saved do not have that right. We can intercede for them.

Intercession is asking on behalf of someone else.

Intercession is actually the technical term for approaching a King. In the Name of Jesus we have been given permission to come before the King of the Universe with our petitions. What an honor! What a privilege!

The prayer of intercession is normally used when praying for the lost. But the Holy Spirit can also make intercession for the saints as He helps us in our prayer life.

**Romans 8:27** *Now He who searches the hearts knows what the mind of the Spirit is, because He makes intercession for the saints according to the will of God.*

There are believers who are too weak, sick, distracted, beaten down or ignorant of God's word to take advantage of their rights and privileges in Christ. Let's make intercession for them! Let's come before our King and ask on their behalf. Let's get them the help that they need. We have access. We have the right to go to the throne of God 24/7.

## The Prayer of Commitment

The prayer of commitment involves casting our cares, worries and anxieties on the Lord. We let go of them and commit them to Him.

**1 Peter 5:7** *casting all your care upon Him, for He cares for you.*

We cast our cares on the Lord by taking them to Him in prayer and laying them down at His feet.

And we leave them there.
    We entrust them to Him.
        We don't pick them back up and take them with us.
            We refuse to worry.

Worrying doesn't help anyone nor does it change anything. Actually worry is a sin because Jesus said, "Don't worry!"

**Matthew 6:25** *Therefore I say to you, do not worry about your life*

**Matthew 6:31** *Therefore do not worry*

**Matthew 6:34** *Therefore do not worry about tomorrow,*

Don't worry,
    don't worry,
        don't worry!

How does this apply to prayer?

Worrying is meditating on fear and fear is the opposite of faith. If we are worrying, then apparently we don't believe that God has heard our prayers. We don't believe that we received the thing we asked for!

Many people pray but as soon as they say "amen" they start worrying about the situation they just finished praying about! That will undo the effects of our prayers and defeat us every time! Cast all of your cares, worries and anxieties on the Lord. Commit them to Him. Let Him carry them for you. If you are carrying them, then He can't carry them for you!

What should we do instead of worrying?

"Don't worry - be happy!" ☺

Not bad advice really.

Better yet, "Don't worry! Pray and commit your cares to Him!"

Pray and give thanks and then like Paul said, *"The peace of God, which surpasses all understanding, will guard your hearts and minds through Christ Jesus!"* **(Philippians 4:7)**

## The Prayer of Consecration

The prayer of consecration is submitting our will to the will of God. Jesus is the best example for this prayer. He prayed in the Garden of Gethsemane and said, *"Not my will, but Yours, be done."*

Although we can't pray this prayer for anyone else, the principle is still useful when praying for others.

For example, we might think that we know what is best for someone else –

Like our children,
　　　　or our spouse,
　　　　　　　or our church
　　　　　　　　　　or our pastor.

But we don't know everything. Unless we are praying a specific promise or principle of God for someone else, it is advisable to use the "Not my will, but Yours, be done" clause. God has plans and purposes for everyone. Sometimes we know what they are and sometimes we don't. We know it's His will to heal, deliver, provide and bless but we don't always know if they should live here or there or somewhere else!

When we don't know what His plans for someone else are, we shouldn't pray as if we did know. We can pray what we think is best but we have to add, "Yet not my will but Yours be done."

Maybe we want our children to go a certain college
    or maybe we want our spouse to apply for a certain job
      or maybe we think our church or pastor
        should start a new program or ministry.

But maybe what we want isn't the right thing.

Don't be like the pastor who partially quoted Jeremiah 29:11 to one of his church members and said, "I know the plans that I have for you" but then left out the "declares the Lord" part. Plans and purposes come from the Lord – His will not our will.

Consecrate your will and your desires to the Lord and He will make sure that all things work together for good!

## The Prayer of Worship and Thanksgiving

This one needs no explanation! Praise and worship are the highest forms of prayer! One thing is sure, if we would thank and praise God more, we would certainly do less worrying. I also believe that if we'd spend more time praising, thanking and worshipping God, we'd have to do far less asking and begging.

As I said, there are many good books written about the different kinds of prayer and it's not my intention to go into all of that in this book. However, we should make use of all the various kinds of prayer when we're praying for believers.

## Praying in the Spirit

*Ephesians 6:18 And pray in the Spirit on all occasions with all kinds of prayers and requests. With this in mind, be alert and always keep on praying for all the Lord's people.*

When praying for all the Lord's people, we are told to pray all kinds of prayer as the Holy Spirit leads us. The Holy Spirit will lead us to pray in the way that most effectively addresses the needs of those for whom we are praying.

Thank God for the Holy Spirit!

He helps us in our prayer life. We know so little but He knows so much! He knows everything! There are times when we don't know what we should ask. (**Romans 8:26**) We know that someone needs help but what he or she truly needs may be a mystery to us.

The Holy Spirit knows exactly what they need! He will help us pray. He will reveal things to us. He will give us words of knowledge and words of wisdom! **(1 Corinthians 12:8)** He will speak to our hearts and pray through our lips.

Praying in the Spirit also includes praying in other tongues. If you disagree with that statement, feel free to just skip over the next few lines. Just don't forget that you still have to love me even if you have a different opinion about it! It's a command! ☺

When we don't know what God's will is in a certain situation – or when "what we should pray for" is a mystery to us – the Holy Spirit can give us utterance in tongues! There's that word utterance again.

***Acts 2:4*** *And they were all filled with the Holy Spirit and began to speak with other tongues, as the Spirit gave them utterance.*

Great word, utterance! ☺

When we are filled with the Spirit we will speak in tongues. Speaking in tongues was the first of the nine spiritual gifts given to the church. It is a gift that has many purposes and can greatly enrich our prayer life!

***1 Corinthians 14:2*** *For he who speaks in a tongue does not speak to men but to God, for no one understands him; however, in the spirit he speaks mysteries.*

Some think that the gift of tongues was used only as a sign to unbelievers. But the gift is actually called "varieties of tongues" and is multifaceted. It has many purposes and uses.

At times it was used as a sign but here in **1 Corinthians 14:2** Paul is referring to *praying* in other tongues. "In the spirit he speaks to God". Speaking to God is praying.

And check this out: The person speaking in tongues is said to be speaking "mysteries". They are mysteries to the speaker but they are not mysteries to God.

The Holy Spirit will help us pray when we don't know what to pray for as we should.

For us it's a mystery – for Him it is not.

There may be groanings and sighings as in **Romans 8:26** or there may be various kinds of tongues – but whatever form it takes – yield yourself to the Holy Spirit in prayer. He helps us in our weaknesses and inadequacies. He will help us pray out mysteries. He will give us words to pray about things for which we have no words of our own.

*1 Corinthians 14:14 For if I pray in a tongue, my spirit prays, but my understanding is unfruitful.*

Praying in tongues is spirit prayer. Your spirit, inspired by the Holy Spirit begins to pray in a language that you never learned. Paul said that when he prayed in tongues his mind didn't understand what he was praying.

I don't always understand everything that I am praying in tongues.

This is biblical.

But even though I don't understand, the Holy Spirit who is inspiring me does. What should we do then?

Glad you asked. So is Paul.

*1 Corinthians 14:15 What is the conclusion then? I will pray with the spirit, and I will also pray with the understanding. I will sing with the spirit, and I will also sing with the understanding.*

Pray with your own language – with your understanding - AND pray in tongues. Not one or the other but both!

Again, my spiritual father used to say, "I pray as far as I can with my understanding and when I sense that there's more that needs to be prayed, I pray in tongues."

By praying in other tongues we can be sure that we are praying the perfect will of God for our brothers and sisters in Christ. Make use of this valuable gift when praying for believers.

Praying in tongues will
>   edify you,
>>     build you up,
>>>       and strengthen you
>>>>         in your most holy faith! (**Jude 1:20**)

It is also a praise language and a wonderful way to thank God. (See **1 Corinthians 14:15-17**) I don't know about you but sometimes I have a praise in my heart that is bigger than my vocabulary can express. Sometimes there's gratitude so huge that saying "Thank You Father" a thousand times wouldn't be able to express just how thankful I am. These are great times to praise and thank God in other tongues!

Jesus said that speaking in new tongues is a sign that should accompany all believers!

**Mark 16:17** *And these signs will follow those who believe: In My name they will cast out demons; they will speak with new tongues*

Jesus said it.
I believe it.
It's good!

Let's get back to Ephesians 6:18.

**Ephesians 6:18** *praying always with all prayer and supplication in the Spirit, being watchful to this end with all perseverance and supplication for all the saints*

Another important principle found in this scripture is perseverance in prayer. This word perseverance means to continue steadfastly in a thing. It also means to give unremitting care. In other words pray and keep praying.Never give up.

As we already noted, some situations require that we pray more than once – especially situations that are dependent upon someone else's will. If someone needs to make a decision or make a change in their lives, you may have to persevere a while.

God never gives up on people and we shouldn't either!

***Romans 8:26-27** Likewise the Spirit also helps in our weaknesses. For we do not know what we should pray for as we ought, but the Spirit Himself makes intercession for us with groanings which cannot be uttered. 27 Now He who searches the hearts knows what the mind of the Spirit is, because He makes intercession for the saints according to the will of God.*

Charles Finney wrote much about the spirit of prayer. The spirit of prayer is the Holy Spirit inspiring and motivating us to pray. Sometimes we sense a genuine burden for someone. Sometimes we know what it is and sometimes we don't. We just know that someone needs prayer. We can take that burden to the Lord. We can pray it through. We can prevail in prayer with the Holy Spirit's help!

I have heard testimonies about how this Spirit-led prayer actually saved people who were in great danger or who were lying on their deathbed!

One day when I was working in my painting business, the spirit of prayer came upon me. Suddenly I had a burden to pray. I knew it was urgent. It felt like a weighty, pressing need mixed with deep agony and desperation and it flooded my heart! I had no idea of who the Lord wanted me to pray for or what they needed. All I knew is that I had to pray!

Thankfully, I was working alone in a house and could just drop everything and pray. God knows when we are available and when we are not.

I got on my knees and began to pray. I prayed in tongues and with groans and deep sighs. It felt like my insides were going to come up right out of my mouth. (I know that sounds disgusting but that's what it felt like!) This prayer came from the very depths of my being. I prayed in the spirit for about 20 – 30 minutes and then the burden lifted. I felt relief in my spirit. Joy and thanksgiving replaced the burden.

Later – that same day in the evening – I got a telephone call from a brother who lived more than a thousand miles away. We had been good friends and attended the same church before I moved. He told me that his wife had left him and their five children. He said that he was broken hearted and that he had been fighting with thoughts of suicide. He went on to tell me that earlier in the day he had been tempted to take his own life.

It was at the same time that the spirit of prayer came upon me!

When the Spirit of prayer comes upon you – or when you sense that deep burden to pray – hit your knees as soon as you can and join forces with the Holy Spirit in intercession! It might make the difference between life and death for a brother or sister!

Thank God for the leading of the Holy Spirit!

Just to be clear on the matter, prayer doesn't always have to be a burden or filled with groans and sighings! Prayer can also be a great joy!

Prayer can and should normally be an uplifting and encouraging time with the Lord. He has given us promises. There's joy in His presence. We fellowship with the One who loves us. We are spending time with the One Who gave Himself for us and Who has promised to always be there for us!

If your prayer times are burdensome, boring and bland you probably aren't praying right. Here are two tips that will change your prayer life into times of refreshing.

- Add more praise and worship to your prayers! (Lots more!)
- Pray much in other tongues.

Stop asking and begging and start thanking and praising. And when you run out of words, let the Holy Spirit give you utterance in tongues. There is a refreshing that comes from praying in tongues that you can't get anywhere else! More utterance Lord!

Surely, there are times for groans but here's a scripture that some of us groaners need!

***Philippians 1:3-4*** *I thank my God upon every remembrance of you, Always in every prayer of mine for you all making request* *with joy*

Paul made his requests with joy!
We can make our requests with joy!

What made Paul joyful?

First of all, the presence of God made him joyful!

**Psalm 16:11** *You will show me the path of life; In Your presence is fullness of joy; At Your right hand are pleasures forevermore.*

There is joy in the presence of God! God is omnipresent – He's present everywhere – but He doesn't always *manifest* His presence everywhere. He manifests His presence where people praise and worship Him.

**Psalm 22:3** *But You are holy, Enthroned in the praises of Israel.*

God dwells in the praises of His people! He reveals His presence when we worship Him. His presence becomes tangible as we praise Him. You can sense His presence. You can feel His presence.

Praise Him and the atmosphere changes.
Joy comes.
Peace comes.
Strength comes!

**Nehemiah 8:10** Do not sorrow, for the joy of the Lord is your strength."

We come before the Lord with praise and thanksgiving. He manifests His presence and dwells in our praises. There's joy in His presence and that joy makes us strong! Prayer time should be an edifying time!

Like I said, there are times when a burden of prayer may come upon us. I've been there and know what it's like. Sometimes you can only groan or weep or pray in tongues. But we need to pray that burden through! We need to pray until that burden lifts.

When we have "prayed through" there's going to be a note of victory. Joy will fill our hearts! Our strength will be renewed and we will stand up confidently knowing that God has heard our prayer and answered positively.

Paul made his requests for the Philippian believers with joy because there's joy in God's presence. Another reason for his great joy was because he prayed in faith. He knew God would hear and answer! Genuine faith is accompanied by two main characteristics – joy and peace!

**Romans 15:13** *Now may the God of hope fill you with all joy and peace in believing, that you may abound in hope by the power of the Holy Spirit.*

Confidently knowing that God has heard our prayers fills us with joy and peace! Faith is more than a confident persuasion that God is ABLE to do all that He promised. It is being completely convinced that He WILL do all that He promised! If we believe Him, impossibilities disappear!

All things are possible with God!
All things are possible to those who believe!
(That'll make you happy if you're a believer.)

Another reason Paul could make his requests with joy is because he connected the request with thanksgiving. (Not the holiday with turkey and pumpkin pie but giving thanks to God.) Connect your requests to thanksgiving. Don't just ask. Ask and give thanks!

Father I ask You
And I thank You
Thank You for hearing
Thank You for answering
Thank You for providing
Thank You for healing
Thank You for restoring
Thank You for working
Thank You for helping
Thank You! Thank You! Thank You!

Additionally, Paul genuinely loved the people that he was praying for. They had been a blessing to him and just thinking about them made him happy! Do you have people like that in your life? Make some joyful requests on their behalf.

But even if the people we are praying for don't always make us happy, giving thanks to God for them will fill us with joy. When we give thanks we are choosing to look for thankworthy things. We are choosing to love. Love believes the best of people!

Every choice and decision we make to love people will bring joy to our hearts.

It might not always be the laughing, giddy kind of joy but it will be a joy that has great depth of meaning!

I believe that most of our prayer time should be a joyous time. I believe that God wants to strengthen us when we pray. I believe He wants to reward us as we diligently seek Him!

**Hebrews 11:6** *But without faith it is impossible to please Him, for he who comes to God must believe that He is, and that He is a rewarder of those who diligently seek Him.*

There is a reward for the pray-er, for the seeker, for the one who comes to God in faith! God wants us to believe that He will reward us every time we come to Him. He actually demands that we believe He's going to bless us when we seek Him in faith!

We MUST believe that He is
AND we MUST believe that He'll reward us.

He IS a rewarder!
That's not just what He does.
That's who He is!

Start to see God as your Rewarder instead of your slave driver. He wants to bless you and reward you with good things!

He rewards us with His presence.
He rewards us with answered prayer.
He rewards us with His help in our times of need!

The apostle John tells us that we should be confident in our prayer life! If we pray according to God's will we can confidently know that He hears us!

**1 John 5:14** *Now this is the confidence that we have in Him, that if we ask anything according to His will, He hears us. 15 And if we know that He hears us, whatever we ask, we know that we have* *the petitions that we have asked of Him.*

We know that He hears us and we know that we have it!

If we pray according to His word, we are praying according to His will. His word is His will! One aspect of His will is to make praying for our brothers and sisters in Christ a priority!

Hallelujah! Praying God's Word in faith always gets heard and answered! If we really believe this, we're going to be making lots of joyful requests!

I remember when I started acting upon priority number one in prayer.

### It was fun!

I prayed the **Ephesians 3:14-21** prayer and just had to rejoice knowing that God was hearing and answering! I prayed, "Lord strengthen my brothers and sisters in Christ by your Spirit in their inner man! Wherever they are and whatever they're doing right now, I pray that they'd sense your strength and power coming upon them!"

My confidence was so great that I could actually imagine their faces lighting up! I could imagine burdens being lifted and strength filling their hearts! It was almost as if I could see how the Holy Spirit was quickening them and moving in their lives at that very moment! What a joy! What a blessing to know that people are being helped!

Let's get some joy in our prayer life. We can rejoice knowing that our Father wants to answer our prayers.

He wants to bless us and minister to our brothers and sisters in Christ even more than we want Him to! Glory to God!

There is a place of fellowship with the Father
    and cooperation with the Holy Spirit
        in the Name of Jesus
            that is the most wonderful,
                fulfilling, joy-filled place
                    you will ever experience
                        here on planet earth.

It is the place of Spirit led, Spirit filled and Scripture based prayer.

The door to heaven is open and God is calling us to take our place in prayer!

# 13. CONCLUSION

I pray that this book has encouraged and inspired you to pray for the body of Christ more than ever. I pray that you will become a committed "priority number one" pray-er.

I am persuaded that if we will make prayer for the body of Christ priority number one in our prayer lives, we will see powerful results. I believe revival will come. I believe our churches will experience renewal and great favor. I believe our leaders will be strengthened and hear from God. I believe that the world will see that we belong to Jesus and recognize that living for Jesus is the best thing in the world!

I am fully persuaded that when they see our love for one another and the goodness of God in our midst, they will start knocking on our doors and asking how they can be a part of this most wonderful, glorious and precious thing called the church!

*1 Timothy 3:15 but if I am delayed, I write so that you may know how you ought to conduct yourself in the house of God, which is the church of the living God, the pillar and ground of the truth.*

The church is the pillar and foundation of truth in our world and in our communities. Whether they know it or not, they need us. When the body of Christ is strong and blessed, our communities will be blessed and reached for the cause of Christ.

Strengthen the pillars and foundations!
Strengthen this glorious house of the living God with your prayers!

And remember, when you place God's kingdom in position number one on your prayer list, He has promised to add to you all the things that you need. Priority number one is an unselfish expression of love that will cause your love to grow and more love to flow to you.

I think of it as a prayer revolution. It may go against some of what we have heard or have been doing in our prayer lives.

But it's the word of God!
Believe it.
Act upon it.

Be a priority number one pray-er and praise God as you see your church change, your community change and your world impacted for the cause of Christ.

I believe that the Lord is saying,

"Bless My family.
Reach out to My children!
My heart longs for them to walk
in the liberating light of My redemption.
I want them to know the depth, height, length and breadth
of My never ending love for them!
I want them to be strong and successful,
filled with joy and with My Spirit!
I want their marriages and families
to experience some of heaven on earth!
I want their businesses, careers and ministries
to be prosperous, fulfilling and fruitful!
I want them to shine like bright lights
in the darkness of the world!
I want the nations to see my glory
and goodness in their lives!
I have provided all that they need for a
life of abundance and significance!
Help each other, My children!
Pray for one another!
Together you can do it.
Together you are stronger!"

And to that I say, "Amen

# ABOUT THE AUTHOR

Fred Lambert was born the first time in 1960. He was born again in 1984. In the same year he married the love of his life, the beautiful and noble Judy. They have two grown children – Joshua and Hannah, a daughter in-love – Irene, two wonderful grandchildren – Joy and Noah, and a son in-love – Kevin. Fred plays guitar and piano, sings, writes songs and loves to worship. He has recorded three albums. He is the founder of Fred Lambert Ministries, a non-profit international missions organization. He is pastor of the Freie Christengemeinde Wels (Free Christian Church Wels) in Austria where he's lived since 1994. He and Judy are the national directors for Rhema Bible Training College Austria. His favorite color is blue. His favorite ice-cream is pistachio. His favorite food is the world famous "Philly Cheesesteak Hoagie". His favorite holiday is Christmas. His favorite sport is baseball and his favorite superhero is Jesus!

You can visit Fred at www.fredlambert.net.

Made in the USA
Monee, IL
06 February 2023